Am I Invisible?

Am I Invisible?

Things
I Wish Teachers
Knew

MURPHY LYNNE

gatekeeper press

Columbus, Ohio

Am I Invisible? Things I Wish Teachers Knew

Published by Gatekeeper Press
2167 Stringtown Rd, Suite 109
Columbus, OH 43123-2989
www.GatekeeperPress.com

ISBN (paperback): 9781662901782
eISBN: 9781662901775

Dedication

I would like to thank these teachers who continually held space for me. Thank you. It meant more to me than you will ever know. Mrs. Jennings, Mrs. Hobbs, Mrs. Lichti, Mrs. Gawith, Mrs. Jenkins, Mrs. Whetstone, Mr. Foster, Mrs. Ferguson, Mrs. Ryan, Mrs. Huscher, Mrs. Endicott, Mr. Cornelson, and Mr. Dusenbery.

I would like to dedicate this book to both of my grandfathers who have passed away. They were creators and mentors, both in their own ways, and I did not understand or appreciate the gifts that were offered in their work until they passed. Creativity and mentorship is a form of art. My grandfather passed right before I began writing this book. The last time I saw him healthy was at my high school graduation, which was a really big deal for me. He was an artist and impacted a lot of people. I did not realize how much of an impact he had until he passed.

I believe writing is a form of art, and it has aided me in pursuing my creativity as well as sharing a story. A story that I hope will impact tons of people in the best of ways. My grandparents both taught me what it is like to create, whether it be with pen and paper, with your hands, or helping people in the physical form. We all have the power to create something beautiful.

My family has been my constant support system throughout my life and throughout this whole process. My mom has helped tremendously in putting this piece together for you all to read. I love you, Mom and Dad. Thank you for always being there for me.

Contents

Don't look away! Don't ignore those kids that are harder to connect with. While these kids may not want to be in the spotlight, no one, and I mean *NO ONE*, truly wants to be invisible. A smile can take the right child through an entire day!

CHAPTER 1

My Truth

It is seventh grade, and I am walking into the cafeteria for the one hundred and seventh time this year. It is the one hundred and seventh time that I want to be anywhere but here. It is the one hundred and seventh time that my stomach is in a knot. It is the one hundred and seventh time that my heart is racing. It is the last place I want to be. It is the worst part of my day. I see all of the kids joking with each other, pushing each other, having fun, talking. How do they do that? I wish I could do that.

I stand in line, looking down at my feet, the back of the kid's head in front of me, looking anywhere except in someone else's eyes. I get my food and make my way through the line. I am good with this taking a long time. The longer it takes, the longer I have until the real terror of finding a place to sit. The actual worst part of the day.

I go through the line and put in my lunch number without a word to anyone, including the lunch ladies, and they don't really say anything to me either. It is time. My heart is racing.

I hate this more than I can say. I turn to see everyone at their tables. No one makes eye contact with me; it feels intentional, although it probably isn't. I want to run, but I don't. I want to leave, but I do not (I am not allowed). I want someone to give me a smile or wave me over, the way I see them do to others, but they don't. Instead, I sit at the nearest empty table. It is quick. It is safe. No one will look at me, like, "Why is she sitting here?" I won't have to make conversation. I can just be, even if it feels bad. I can get through this. Twenty more minutes. I can do this.

There are teachers in the room. Supervisors—do they notice me? Do they see me? Am I actually invisible?

Who are you? Are you a kid who wants to be invisible? Are you a kid who feels invisible but does not want to be? Are you a kid who feels trapped in the cycle and does not know how to escape to be seen and heard?

Are you a teacher? Have you ever noticed the students who look like they want to be invisible? I was one of those students. For a long time, I thought being invisible would make things easier. School was hard for me, socially and academically. Making myself invisible would make it better, right? Wrong, as it turns out. It took years to find out how wrong that assumption was.

When I figured out that being invisible wasn't great, I didn't know how to change it. As a student, I was incredibly vulnerable. I needed teachers—and good ones! Throughout my education, I had some great ones, some good ones, and some that truly failed me. I felt a sense of obligation to write this book, not only for teachers but for those students who have not yet found their voice. I remember I so badly wished that my teachers had this information, because maybe then my story would have turned out a little differently. This is what I wish teachers knew throughout my years spent in school as a kid who was high-functioning on the autism spectrum, introverted, and with the inevitable anxiety and depression that followed.

> *"I have come to the frightening conclusion that I am the decisive element. It is my personal approach that creates the climate. It is my daily mood that makes the weather.*
>
> *I possess a tremendous power to make life miserable or joyous. I can be a tool of torture or an instrument of inspiration. I can humiliate, hurt, or heal. In all situations, it is my response that decides whether a crisis is escalated or de-escalated, and a person is humanized or de-humanized. If we treat people as they are, we make them worse. If we treat people as they ought to be, we help them become what they are capable of becoming."*
>
> Haim Ginott – Author, *Teacher and Child: A Book for Parents and Teachers, 1972*

When I first saw this quote, the words were taped on the wall of a day-care center I worked at. It spoke to me with such force that I felt as if there was fire surging throughout my whole body. The little girl inside of me attempted to yell as loud as she could because *those* words were what she so fiercely ached to speak. Those words are what this book embodies. The truth that deserves to be spoken and which should be recognized as a catalyst for understanding. Most importantly, my hope is that this book leads to the change that could occur through these powerful words and my own truth. It provides me with an immeasurable amount of hope not only for teachers but for the students who I know are sitting alongside me.

I have always loved to write; it became an outlet in which I began to express the deepest parts of myself. Writing many blog posts, poetry, and just being the average journaler, I had a voice. A voice that I never could express in any other form besides pen and paper. Originally, I did not plan to explain the backstory of how and why teachers or school affected me as deeply as they did. I soon realized this is a story, whether it be mine or someone else's, that I believe teachers and those who don't quite fit in need to hear. My story is not sunshine and rainbows, nor is it all darkness. I have amazing parts that I am proud of, as well as dark parts that took me a long time to not be ashamed of.

This is the reality that happens to students like me. I believe teachers need to be more aware of the effects their words and actions have and the domino effect that follows. My goal is to talk about some of the stereotypes surrounding students like me and destigmatize them. Let's talk frankly. This book is also for me to feel a sense of peace, confronting my difficult time in school while hiding behind a pen.

After graduating high school, I spent a lot of time reflecting. Reflecting on everything that I have gone through, inside and outside school doors. Graduating was more than receiving a diploma or passing all of my required classes; it symbolized a journey that I fought like hell to get through. During that time of reflection, I got an overwhelming urge to write. I felt as though I could not keep everything that I had learned inside; I had to let it out for others to hear. This is my way of expressing my voice, the best way I know how.

Teachers can change a child's story.

This starts with INTENTIONAL CONVERSATIONS. Have them frequently, with eye contact and genuine tone. Keep up this consistent effort—it is worth it—even if you are uncomfortable at first because students don't respond in the typical way. Teachers truly seeing students makes it more possible for other students to accept one another!

CHAPTER 2

The Early Years: Childhood

As early as when I was in the womb, I have always been somewhat of an experiment. I started in a petri dish, an odd thing to envision, but it is, in fact, true. My mom still has the dish that I started in when she went through in vitro fertilization. I grew in this dish—eight cells to twelve cells to thirty-two cells. Three embryos were worthy of being placed in my mom's uterus for a real chance at life. Not saying the other two weren't tough enough, but let's just say I am not a triplet. Thank God I'm not a triplet, for my parents' sake.

I was the embryo that survived—a sole survivor, you could say. This seems to be true for the first part of my life— alone but surviving. I am and have always been a puzzle that no one can seem to find the correct pieces to. After all it took to conceive me, I was born three months premature, at twenty-six weeks' gestation. My mother had preeclampsia, a condition causing dangerously high blood pressure, and the only cure was to deliver.

I was born on August 13, 1998, weighing one pound, eight ounces, and equivalent to the length of a ruler. I spent the next three months in the neonatal intensive care unit (NICU), fighting to make a statement that I was here to stay. From birth, I was very strong-willed and determined, from graduating out of the NICU to finally learning how to walk and talk, to fighting my way through my teenage years. I was fighting to make a statement that I was enough exactly as I am. Something that I doubted very deeply along the way, many times.

I had some level of services from birth, such as occupational, physical, and speech therapy, helping me learn how to suck from a bottle, with speech, and with fine and gross motor skills. I began preschool at the age of three and stayed in that classroom for three years. The last two years, I grew a relationship with my teacher, Miss Julia, and was very close to her, as close as a three-year-old gets. My parents treated me like a normal child because, for all they knew, I was. They knew there were some "unique qualities," such as my weird obsession with lining up my Disney *Bear in the Big Blue House* figurines on repeat for hours and completely losing my mind if one got out of place.

I had a strong aversion to textures. For example, I loved my family pet kitty but only pretended to pet him because the feel of the fur would send me into shivers and chills, breaking out into what my parents called "straight arming." Straight arming was something I involuntarily did to show that I was unhappy when things didn't go my way.

I also had sensory issues that caused a need for my parents to brush my hands and arms to desensitize me. Picture brushing a dog to tame its shedding. My parents did this with a surgical scrub brush. Eventually, a question was posed to them that stuck in the back of my parents' minds until I was officially diagnosed. My preschool teacher asked my mom after she picked me up one day if they had ever considered testing me for Asperger's Syndrome. Miss Julia believed it was more than the developmental delays often seen from my premature birth.

My mom was familiar with autism and Asperger's Syndrome, as she was an elementary school principal. She respectfully took the feedback but told me years later that they didn't proceed with testing because there was nothing that she would do differently with me, whether I was diagnosed on the autism spectrum or not. They would make accommodations but did not think they needed a diagnosis to do so. I do not blame my mom for this, because no parent wants to believe there is something wrong with their child, but part of me does wonder if having that diagnosis earlier in my childhood would have made a positive impact in the school environment. My mom, in hindsight, has since shared with me that not getting the diagnosis earlier remains one of her biggest regrets. A diagnosis makes a difference in a teacher's ability to understand the challenges a child may face and therefore address them in the correct way.

Until fourth grade, I attended the same elementary school where my mom worked. My mom became the head leader in school and at home. Those couple of years were the best experiences I have ever had in school, and I still remember them fondly. I had a handful of good friends and had a really good connection with my teachers, which may only have been because I was the principal's daughter, but nonetheless, I felt special. I felt as if they actually cared about what I had to say.

Looking back, I remember more of my younger childhood years because I felt truly myself, with no thought attached. Symptoms of the autism spectrum surfaced in those early years, with a couple of events raising red flags. I had a thing for sand, and I mean a *real* thing. I was obsessed. The first thing I did at recess was head to the sand. I liked the texture, and it was a solitary activity that I had control over. I didn't have to worry about who I would play with or being included; I could just be.

One red-flag incident involved a little rubber lizard named Roger who I was obsessed with, and luckily, my friend Kate also joined in on the fun. We took him to the playground with us and even played babysitter at each other's houses, caring for him. It felt good to be accepted for something I knew, in hindsight, was a little off, and to have a partner in crime.

Kate and I were heartbroken when we lost Roger in our huge school building a couple months later. Some may say that is just kids being kids, but I believe that was part of my disorder rearing its head, as well as my social anxiety beginning to surface. In third grade, the teacher (who I truly loved) had us take turns reading a sentence of a book during library circle time. This is my earliest memory of my anxiety starting.

There were about twenty students, and we were going around the circle, taking turns reading paragraphs. When it came to my turn, I could not get the words out, not because I could not read the text, but because I physically could not speak from fear.

Before that moment, I didn't even know this fear existed. I remember the librarian rubbing my back and telling me, "Just read the words." Subconscious anxiety, if that exists.

I do not recall any physical symptoms from anxiety in elementary school, other than in third grade when I could not utter the words from a book. But I was uncomfortable in my own skin. Did it start there? Had it been a part of me that I wasn't aware of? Were other people noticing? Or was I invisible? At that age, I didn't want to be invisible. I would save that desire for middle school when things got rough. One strategy was focusing on material things, such as Roger the lizard. Having things to focus on was my way of dealing with it, even if the need for control slowly became apparent, now that I look back on it.

While I was most comfortable in the background, there were times in my childhood that I took on roles and activities that put me directly in the spotlight. This included one of my last experiences at my mom's school. I am not sure if I could sing or if my family just convinced me I could. (I was definitely convinced.) The school held a talent show each year—auditions and all. My mom really wanted me to try out, and I thought, why not—maybe I was good enough. Maybe this was my thing—singing.

I loved the thought that I might be good enough; this would feel good. I made it through the auditions, maybe just because my mom was the principal, but regardless, I was in. Now it was a different animal altogether. I would actually have to get up in front of everyone—750 kids, staff, and all of the parents who came to see the show. I was singing "Tomorrow" from the musical Annie. My mom got an orphan outfit from one of the teachers, and we practiced. I felt pretty good about it and was ready but nervous about showtime.

My mom was the MC for the show, and she was busy doing all of her principal duties to get ready. I was sure I could do it and was kind of excited. I was after the violin solo. My mom introduced my act and said I was her daughter. I stepped out onto the high school stage and knew, beyond the lights, was a sea of people. My mom was in the wings, watching. I started, sounding pretty good. This was going to be the moment that the quiet girl was going to slay the stage and show everyone what I was capable of Not so fast! A little over halfway through, I froze! I couldn't remember the words. My mom moved and hid behind the piano, trying to get my attention to mouth the words as a reminder. My heart racing, anxiety swallowed me up. I couldn't focus on the next line. It was getting awkward, and it quickly became clear that I was done. Everyone started clapping for me. This was confusing for me because I knew that I wasn't done. Despite the disaster, the clapping felt good. It was for me. I actually wasn't bad in the moments I wasn't frozen.

My mom immediately ran backstage, devastated for me. She only wanted to make me feel better, forgetting that she was the MC of the show. This made for an even more awkward situation. They had to come get my mom and remind her—seriously, she forgot she was part of the show. The show must go on, right? This would not be my last attempt at getting up in front of others, but it was my first attempt that went terribly wrong.

Roger wasn't my only obsession. *Dolls*! I couldn't get enough of them. They were my safety, my comfort, and my friends. There were multiple times during my obsession with my lizard and my dolls where I needed everything to be perfect. If the lizard was not wrapped up correctly in his little bed I set up for him, I would feel like I needed to fix it immediately. Interestingly enough, that perfectionistic tendency did not transfer to anything else until later. Nonetheless, being in third grade was the beginning of the end in a way. The last year when I felt as secure in myself as I've ever felt. The last year I felt like I belonged.

Mrs. Jennings, my teacher, was part of this. Back to the facts: teachers make a difference. My kindergarten through second-grade teachers were wonderful, but Mrs. Jennings, she was different. She was one of the first to make a lasting positive impression because she seemed to understand me. She *saw* me. I was not invisible to her, and in turn, she made me not invisible to others. It was powerful, the impact she had on me and my interactions with others. I will forever be grateful for that year and the safety she provided for me.

In elementary school, you have one designated teacher. For students like me, it was very special because they were able to really get to know me and not create assumptions. I felt a connection with my elementary teachers because it was more personal in the way that we got to communicate one-on-one. There is more time in an elementary classroom to create that one-on-one relationship. I believe I built my confidence around connection in my middle elementary years. I knew it was important, but that didn't make achieving the connection any easier. In elementary school, I did not have to hide, nor did I feel like I needed to because my teachers understood me or at least made an amazing effort to do so. Is it possible they were faking this understanding? It didn't matter, because they looked at me, looked me in the eye, and made personal comments to me. They complimented me. They noticed me.

By that point, my mom had two other children, which made the commute even more hectic. Our house was forty minutes away, and trying to get kids out the door took even longer. Having all of us dressed and out the door and dropping my two younger brothers off at day care to get to school by 7:30 in the morning became too much. My mom loved the district, as did I, but there came a point where the commute was making or breaking the decision to stay or move closer.

By the end of the school year, my mom made the decision that we would move to the district closer to our house. That meant leaving my best friend, as well as the connection I had with everyone at the school, including the staff. Losing that connection to the school, teachers, and my best friend Kate, began a downward slide into the spectrum, as well as the introversion that, as a young adult, I am just learning how to navigate.

I don't think you ever realize how much you rely on others, whether it be familiar or a material object, until it suddenly slips from your grasp. The beginning of the fourth grade in my new school was me in my rawest form. I didn't realize how insecure I really was until all I was familiar with disappeared. I had two neighborhood friends who I enjoyed playing with, no doubt, but for the first time, I began to recognize how truly alone I felt. I spent fourth grade kind of in my own bubble, doing schoolwork and just trying to be like all the others. Again, *trying* to be like the others when I was anything but. The anxiety that was surfacing would define my schooling and make a significant impact. What I know now, but unfortunately did not know then, is that it is completely okay, more than okay, to *not* be like the others. If only I had known to embrace who I was sooner. If only I had

had teachers at every turn who celebrated differences, as opposed to working hard to make sure we were all the same.

Unfortunately, I didn't know the answer to that, which is the same dilemma kids find themselves in every day.

I communicated with Kate on a regular basis by calling her after school, which became my daily routine. The two friends I mentioned became more acquaintances as the year went on. I began to recognize how easy it was for them to communicate in class and with other classmates, which was very intriguing because it wasn't as easy for me. The majority of my classmates could raise their hands in order to ask a question or give an answer to the teacher.

I know my teachers expected that I had been taught to raise my hand when I had a question or wanted to participate, but what too many teachers and adults don't realize is that knowing how to do something and actually raising my hand with ease are worlds apart for a kid like me. The other kids could start conversations with those who were sitting beside them like it was nothing. I could not do that. I always wondered how they did that, which is where my deepest insecurities came from. There was a point where I had to have my school counselor work with me on the playground to try to teach me to communicate with others, which was a task, God bless her.

Making friends was a struggle, which only increased my understanding of what the term "insecurity" really meant and felt like. During recess, you would most likely find me in the sand or on the swing. I recognize this now as self-stimulatory behavior, which is also commonly known as stimming or stim. It is very common in autism, especially in lower- functioning cases, but obviously can occur in high-functioning people like me. We have hypersensitive brains, which means we get overstimulated very easily. It can occur from intense excitement, overwhelming emotions, or outward stimuli such as loud noises or an unfamiliar environment. Stimming can range from flapping hands, vocal noises or sounds, to continuous movement. Mine was definitely movement, which explains the swinging. It was a way for me to calm down and escape my reality that I did not understand.

This example of stimming morphed as I got older to include more age-appropriate stimulation such as cartwheeling. I would repeatedly cartwheel around the house, pounding the ground hard with my hands and spinning around again and again. It became the definition of the inward stress I couldn't articulate.

When there was not a swing available at recess, I felt panicked. I did not know what to do. I felt uncomfortable in my own skin, emotionally more than anything. Sitting in my own mind with no stimulation felt wrong and scary. Every day when the time came to go out to recess, I would just pray there would be a swing available because that was my only comfort. On one particular day, other kids got to all the swings before me, and I kid you not, I was like a puppy who could not find its bone. I did not know what to do, so I went and sat next to my teacher, who was walking, scanning the playground.

"You decided not to swing today, huh?" she asked while looking straight ahead as if she was speaking to herself. I nervously laughed and said yes. "You like the swings, don't you?"

I said, "Uh-huh," and slowly walked away, trying to act like I knew what the hell I was going to do next. I have a journal entry from this time that says, "I don't know why I just can't talk to my friends. I just can't."

I remember being amazed at how natural socializing was for my classmates. It is very hard to explain even now; I cannot imagine trying to link the correct words to what I was feeling at that age. In elementary school, I realized bits and pieces of myself that were not like all of my peers, which only fed my insecurity and confusion moving forward. I wish my teacher had taken that conversation a step further, not stating the obvious, but stretching the conversation to build a relationship. I would have given anything to really feel that someone at my new school cared. I knew they were nice, but caring was something different altogether.

Recess is often seen in grade school as a wonderful privilege, which to most students, it very much is. What about those who do not have very many friends, if any? It is almost a setup of sorts. As your peers are running towards the playground, you walk as quickly as you can and attempt to find something to do fast, so you are not seen as the girl who is a loner. I tried my best to redirect the insecurity away from myself by not having anyone to play with, so I did not have enough time to get sad. Not that anyone at that age really seemed to care, but I wanted to be like everyone else, even if I did not know what that exactly looked like. But in fourth grade, I began to disappear. I was becoming invisible.

You might think there is not much a teacher can do in regards to the kids who do not have very many friends to play with at recess. There is some truth to that, of course, in that teachers don't have the power to change a person. But I also believe teachers can create a different story for kids like me with consistent attention and effort and short but intentional conversations. Get beyond "How are you?" See me, know me, get me. Like water dripping can change the shape of a rock, consistent drips from **all** teachers and adults in a building can change a child's shape—for good or bad. You cannot change things overnight, or maybe even at all, but just having that awareness of those possibilities occurring in students can make a difference.

Teachers can make up for a student's loneliness by being there and providing warmth and comfort in place of the friends a student may not have. While many of my teachers were caring, they didn't go out of their way to see or help my emotional needs. They may not have noticed. Was this a side effect of becoming invisible? Is it a teacher's job to notice those that are not seen? I think it is.

At the end of fifth grade, I finally met a friend while I was playing in the sand during recess. It happened pretty organically, sort of like a happy preschooler on the first day of school, kind of easily. My friend traveled with me to middle school, which allowed us to expand our friendship. I also began the roller-coaster of puberty and womanhood at the age of eleven, which was relatively exciting, although it was another somewhat confusing thing that I needed to navigate. I enjoyed the innocence and carefree nature of being that young. The only judgment that occurred was from me, stemming from my own self-built insecurity.

My last year of elementary school was appealing yet terrifying. I remember my last day of fifth grade and the realization that there would be no more recess. How was I going to survive? (I survived.) Ripping my name tag off my desk was as if I was ripping off my innocence. The unknown has always scared me, and transitioning into middle school was no different.

> Don't underestimate the power of a "Hello"! There were teachers who would look at me and say hello. They didn't know it, but that was enough for me to feel safe and believe they might actually like me. You would be surprised how many teachers do not make an effort with kids who are uncomfortable making eye contact, therefore making it easy to be *INVISIBLE*.

CHAPTER 3

The Game-Changer

There is an innocence that you leave behind once you graduate from elementary school. I was now in "big school" with my very own locker, multiple classes to attend, and, most importantly, a lot of new peers. I am grateful that I had a friend to act as my backbone during those first couple months as I acclimated to the new environment of another school. Or at least I thought I did. Some kids change in middle school, and unfortunately, my neighborhood friend was one of them. She suddenly couldn't hang out after school (she literally gave the excuse that she had to wash her hair), have a sleepover, or be bothered to talk to me. I wasn't cool enough for her, I guess. It didn't make sense to me then, and it doesn't make sense to me now. But I do know that it started my middle school off with the lesson that friends aren't necessarily forever—a sad statement that I found to be true time and time again throughout middle and high school.

My sixth-grade year was about as popular as I ever got, and I could not be more grateful for the friends I had and still consider friends to this day (even if we don't talk anymore). I remember my homeroom the most—language arts class. I developed great friendships that meant a lot to me. There were Abigail, Emma, and Sarah. I was the quiet observer that loved to listen to other people's conversations. I believe it is more intriguing to listen to other people's conversations rather than to participate. The four of us were all in the same class but didn't even know it until we had a project in my language arts class. I remember it was an interpretive dance of some sort, having to do with what we were learning. It was a pretty fun project, and it was kind of where I got to know the girls.

I remember I went over to Sarah's house to work on the project with the rest of the group, and she only invited me to sleepover, which was cool. I had to hide my bags so as not to hurt anybody's feelings. We were at each other's houses often, and those were the best times. The friendship felt very authentic. A couple weeks later, I then got put in a two-person group with Emma, and from then on, we were together more than I had ever been with any other friend. The friendship was very real. We got to know each other more, and she always reminded me of how, when we first met, I was so quiet. I just needed someone to give me a chance, although not many did. Once you got to know me, though, I was not all that quiet. The "you are so quiet" description became a recurring theme from teachers, school staff, and my peers who did not get to see the other side of me.

Closer to the end of the semester, the first bomb hit; Abigail was moving. She was one of my neighborhood friends that was always nice, a highlight of sixth grade for me. We were walking to this empty land behind my house that we loved to go to, where we liked to act like we were stranded adventurers. After we were out there a little while, she suggested we stop by this rock because she needed to tell me something. We were with my little brother, so she told him to go "explore" somewhere else.

Abigail then told me quietly that she was moving because of her dad's job. I was shocked. It was totally unexpected, and it shook me up. Neither of us felt like playing our game anymore, so we decided to go back home. Abigail ended up telling my mom while she was sitting at the kitchen table. I am very fortunate that I still had Emma and Sarah with me.

The day that Abigail actually moved was hard, and it was sad not seeing her every day, but it definitely got easier with time. Also, my friendships with Emma and Sarah blossomed. I spent more and more time with them. I was not alone and was included, mainly as an observer, in the pre-teenage world that I was growing up in, which was fun. My friends meant a great deal to me because I knew what it was like to not have any.

Sixth grade was an amazing year regarding friendships, and it was something that I definitely took for granted because meeting someone similar in personality to me and/or actually liking me for me was rare. Which explains why it was such a hard hit when Abigail moved.

I still was loving life with my two best friends. We all really got along well, and I could not have imagined anything better until my world got rocked again. Sarah was moving. Her dad was a pastor and got an opportunity to work at another church. I remember her telling me when we were having a sleepover, and I thought she was kidding. We were soul sisters, essentially, spending many days and nights together with Emma. Sarah was moving in September, and when the day actually came, I had no idea what to do with myself. I was lost. I felt like she was leaving me.

I could feel my anxieties taking control. I would miss our nightly talks with soft music playing on her alarm clock. I would miss making addicting Nutella sandwiches, which she introduced me to. I knew Sarah wasn't dying, but it almost felt like it because she wasn't physically there as my partner in crime anymore—a friend who not only saw me but liked me for me. I learned early on that these types of friends were very rare and should be cherished.

This part of my story is really hard for me to think about, let alone write about. Middle school changed my life in ways that I didn't expect. I know that middle school is a typically tough time for everyone, but the reality is that it was exceptionally rough for me. I feel like I have a buffer between me and this keyboard right now, not allowing me to type.

I don't think I could have prepared myself for how different the two school atmospheres were, starting middle school. Adapting to a new environment took a while to get used to. It was a weird feeling, thinking that most of the teachers cared more for how well you did on a test rather than about getting to know you. You see, maybe to most kids, it is not as important, but for me, it was about whether I could come out of my shell or not. If you are personal with me and act like you are genuinely interested in getting to know me, then I know it is safe enough to slowly do so.

I got to the point where I had to pick and choose which teachers I was comfortable with in terms of communicating with and those who I was not. I did not have to make that choice before, nor did I feel like there was a need to. I was known to every single one of my teachers from preschool until fifth grade. It is different when you only have a specific teacher for forty-five minutes each day, which consists of mostly lectures and independent work. It is difficult to connect when, about five minutes into a lecture, you are debating in your head about asking a simple question. Then you look up at the clock and you realize it's forty minutes later; class is almost over. Did I really spend all that time thinking about one question that takes two seconds to ask? Yes, Murphy, get your shit together. I realized in order to be noticed, you needed to reach out. Unless you were one of those popular kids who got noticed by everyone.

Putting your full attention on one student when you are a teacher is difficult. I am not naive to the fact that there are also twenty others you need to attend to while also attempting to successfully teach the day's lesson. Despite those teachers who may be thinking, "I only have so much time," I am going to state the point anyway. The level of engagement with your students does not have to be a well-thought-out, deep conversation. You received your degree in teaching, not psychology. I realize that. Please don't underestimate the power of simply acknowledging students by saying hello and by making eye contact while they come into the room. That alone would be enough for a kid like me. It seems insignificant, and is typically a gesture we make out of habit, but in my mind, that kind of thing determined if the teacher was nice, liked me, and if I would put in the effort for him or her. It proved the teacher saw me.

Some students may need more one-on-one attention from you, such as sitting next to them while you explain an assignment concept. Being aware of what your students need, and acting accordingly is so beneficial for students in every aspect of their school experience. It allows students to realize that you are genuine and want to help, therefore allowing us to accept the help and nurturing we may be searching for.

Two questions to ask yourself: Are you really listening or just hearing? Are you really engaging or just passing by? Again, never underestimate the power of a hello!

The beginning of seventh grade started out promising and hopeful, with me fantasizing that I could be a part of the popular group. Ha-ha, that is laughable. Nothing could have prepared me for what actually occurred. The sequence of events left me feeling like I was nothing, pulling down my self-worth and self-esteem until there was nothing left. I still cannot pinpoint how it all began; I just remember events happening one by one or rather as twenty things rolled into one. I just watched it go by like a big tangled ball of mishaps. This is a year that I have never talked about in any depth, and even writing this, I can feel my heart speed up a bit. Everything started here.

All my diagnoses started here. My self-worth as a person started here. Getting to know myself from the inside out started here. This part of my story is probably the most vulnerable part. This is where the bottom fell out.

I remember the rest of my seventh-grade year as if I am putting on fogged glasses. I remember bits and pieces, little fragments in time, but none of those bits and pieces make sense. Your brain protects you in times of crisis or trauma, and I believe not recalling details of events helped me do just that. Let's start off from the very beginning: meet your teacher night. Oddly, I remember this fondly. I believe I met my science teacher first. She had curly brown hair, and we made conversation about her yellow lab, which she had a few pictures of. I explained that I also had a lab, except black.

Then I headed over to my language arts classroom. The teacher was organizing her bookshelf as my dad and I walked in; she had big brown eyes and red hair. We seemed to connect really quickly.

Finally, I met my math teacher. He was short, and my friends and I joked about how short he was, along with him being cute, just a little. Later, that giddy laughter and those jokes were muffled with self-consciousness and concern about the verbal attacks he would put me through.

Everything felt normal, normal as in feeling myself, until about a month after Sarah moved. Gradually, I could feel myself become more insecure and withdrawn. I remember feeling off. I was sad, frustrated, and confused because I did not seem to fit in anywhere. Throughout the school year, I knew something wasn't right until I felt like I could not hide it anymore. I guess I wasn't that good at hiding it, because my parents could tell. What I was feeling, I believe, was the depression setting in more so than ever before, but I also knew I was different in school.

It was around this time that I started self-harming—cutting my skin with paper clips and, eventually, scissors. This behavior manifested for many reasons, mostly because I felt incredibly insecure from so many things, and school reinforced to me that

I wasn't good enough. That I wasn't worthy. From other kids ignoring me to my teachers that failed to try to connect to the teacher that seemed to be actively gunning for me—it was a lot. I needed an out. At the time, cutting was an answer. It should never be an answer, but I started to feel desperate. For most, it is hard to understand, but causing myself pain made me feel better, at least in the moment. I had no idea what to do with the social aspect of school, and academically, I already knew I had some developmental delays from the IEP I had since birth. It was a mixture of maturity, realizing how my peers were acting differently than me, becoming aware that it took longer for me to do things, and not feeling as though I could start conversations with them. All that, as well as the many hormones that were swirling through me ... I just knew something was wrong.

One night, I mentioned to my parents what I was feeling and how school was not going as well as I had hoped. I had no idea what depression and anxiety really meant; I just knew what it felt like.

The definitions seemed to fit me pretty closely. My mom and I both felt it was more than just depression and anxiety, so she suggested I get tested for a possible diagnosis on the autism spectrum, which she already had a suspicion of. From then on, I felt like I was a case that no one could quite figure out, being unknowingly watched and analyzed, which I was too naive to realize until I was older. Everyone watched me to see what I would do. I unknowingly became a puzzle, and there was a little piece within me that no one could figure out what the hell to do with.

When I got tested, I walked into the building and saw a therapy dog walking around. She looked like a big poodle. She was my buddy in the waiting room. I had many tests done.

The two I remember the most were the facial expression flash cards and the psychological assessment at the end which, in later years, I would become all too familiar with. The woman asked me what faces corresponded to the emotion, and I pointed to them. I believe I did fairly well with reading facial expressions, but other people may say otherwise.

At the very end was the psychological test. She led me into a very small room with one desk and chair in it. It was a relatively long test, and from these tests, I would receive two more diagnoses which something in me already knew. But I was still taken aback a little.

A week or so later, I got all the tests back, and I was professionally diagnosed with pervasive developmental disorder not otherwise specified (PDD-NOS), which is along the autism spectrum. I learned the spectrum is very diverse. I was also diagnosed with social anxiety and clinical depression. Painful for sure, yet a relief to know, my instincts were correct!

Most people can usually easily pinpoint low-functioning kids because they are clearly showing signs of the disorder. As more studies have come out and more general knowledge is available to the public, we are starting to understand more about how diverse the spectrum really is. People like me appreciate that. From my knowledge and the way my mom sat me down and explained it to me, it works like this: there is a line that has all the disorders ranging from low- to high-functioning autism. Asperger's is one of the high-functioning disorders. Where was I? Well, I am a bit before Asperger's, which is called a pervasive developmental disorder not otherwise specified, which means I am on the spectrum ... but barely. I have some traits that appear to be on it, and also traits that are so-called normal. But nonetheless, I am on it.

I was relieved to have an answer to why I felt different from everyone else, socially and academically, and for why I felt sad the majority of the time. I was relieved to have an answer, and that is all I really cared about.

The impact of receiving an actual name was easier for me to understand. It was a profound moment because I finally had a concrete answer. Therefore, in my head, that provided a possible solution. It took years for me to come to grips with this diagnosis and what it would actually mean to overcome the obstacles. I had a name, but my internal pain was still there. I still was invisible and wanted not to be. How could I change that? I had no idea, and at this point, I didn't know things were going to get more difficult as time went on.

After I received my diagnosis on paper, my mom set up an IEP meeting. There was usually an IEP meeting a couple times a year for all of the teachers to discuss my academic needs. This was an additional meeting to discuss what was going on with me. I did not attend, partially because my mom wanted to speak to my teachers without me in the room, but also because I was ashamed. Ashamed of my diagnosis, because all I wanted was to appear normal to everyone, including my teachers. I believe some of them took what they could and used my vulnerability against me, while others genuinely seemed to care, which I greatly appreciated. It is hard for adults to look past a diagnosis and see a kid who is full of anxiety and one who doesn't have the skill yet to make conversation like the others.

From then on, my IEP meetings up until my senior year of high school were filled with shame because I was embarrassed of who I was.

> Beware of the bullies, and be careful not to become one
> of them!

CHAPTER **4**

Where Everything Changed

My story from here on out may or may not make sense to some. There is so much that happened during this time in my life that I cannot possibly state it as a word-for-word narrative. Some thoughts will be jumbled, weaving in and out of stories. Everything that I am stating here occurred simultaneously with a big ball of confusion within myself which began to fuse together.

One word: cheerleading. I first began my love for cheer when I was eleven. I immediately fell in love with it. I am not talking about girls with skimpy little skirts screaming "let's go" on the sidelines. I'm talking about competitive cheerleading. I started out at the YMCA with a little competition team, and the coach happened to be my cousin, which was kind of cool. I enjoyed it for the time that I was participating, but after about a year or so, I wanted to take on gyms that were a little more competitive. It was a good step in dipping my toes into the cheerleading world, which made me even more confident in participating at a higher-level gym.

This is a sport that is surprising, considering that I am an extreme introvert with a high level of anxiety. Goes to show that regardless of what may seem obvious, obstacles are meant to be overcome and can actually, at times, be of benefit in the most unexpected ways. Being on the mat in a competition was different in that I was anonymous while doing something that gave me purpose and pride. Parents and teachers, don't underestimate what the quiet, on-the-fringe student can be good at. Also, don't underestimate yourself.

I never really thought this would be my thing, and it ended up being something that, in the beginning, gave me a place to belong. I could be somewhat invisible but also seen at the same time. I had a couple competitions under my belt, which is rather humorous to look back on. During a tumbling sequence in the middle of our routine, I froze and totally forgot what I was doing. I looked like a chicken with its head cut off, trying to figure out where I was supposed to go next. I figured it out. We were not the best team in the world, but it was fun, nonetheless.

I quit when my cousin did; seemed like the perfect time to make the transition. A few weeks later, I signed up to be on a competition team at Cheer Fusion. Cheer Fusion quickly became my home away from home and is the best experience I've had in an extracurricular activity.

Being a seventh grader, I got the opportunity to try out for school sports, and what did I choose? You guessed it. The school cheerleading team. I had a little bit of a cocky attitude about it because, in my head, school cheer was way different than the school cheerleading team, so I thought it would be simple. The technique would be simple, anyway. Along with my cocky attitude, I thought maybe this was my chance to finally be the "popular one." I was excited to be involved in the popular chick gossip that I rarely got to hear, as well as to prove that I knew what I was doing.

Let's just say it turned out to be anything but what I internally hoped for. In the end, school cheer was more about fitting in and less about the actual skill. The focus on social importance in school cheer fed my deepest insecurities. I couldn't get out of my head, and sadly, this was another missed opportunity for a teacher to make a difference. Instead, it made me hate myself, so I felt more left out than ever before.

Competitive cheer was my home away from home. A place that I could just get away and let my worries change to pure enjoyment of what I was doing. In a way, the pure excitement and joy that I found through cheerleading is what I believe kept me sane. I do not know what a different place I would be in if I had not had that outlet to run to and be excited about. The gym was the one place where I knew exactly what I was doing. I knew I was good at it, and that provided me with great solace. While I was somewhat invisible in the gym, the girls weren't mean to me at this point.

I was in my second year of competing, and I remember feeling on top of the world. Mainly because I was looked at by the rookies as someone who knew her stuff, which was a new feeling for me. Going into a new season, girls try out, and you get placed on a team based on your skill level. I was one of the veterans on the team, and my coach made that known. Coach Bryan may never know how special this made me feel. Adults working with kids need to take a minute and just say something nice. I might not have shown how great it made me feel inside, but he didn't say it to just get a reaction—he was genuine.

All adults involved with kids need to compliment them intentionally and genuinely; too often, they just don't! I was one of the more flexible students, considering my lack of flexibility just starting out, and Coach Bryan noticed and gave me praise. He was tough, but in the right ways, and I knew that and respected him. Not until a year or so later did he cross the boundary between tough love to just plain mean. This was the downfall of another thing that I loved and made me feel more INVISIBLE.

However, at this point, I was on a team which I felt excited to be a part of, and I was genuinely happy to be there. I loved the atmosphere of it all, the excitement leading up to competitions even if we did have to run five laps every time our stunt fell in practice. The team bonding when we were on that mat with a screaming audience, encouraging each other to keep that damn stunt in the air, was incredible. I loved it and still very much cherish the memories. I am grateful that I was privileged enough to be a part of it.

The gym was the only area in my life where I felt like I could be myself. Where I could be goofy and silly and have fun all at the same time. I became grateful to have a place in which I felt I could do so, because my school life was, unbeknownst to me, falling apart.

I had received a diagnosis I didn't fully understand. I was also still cutting when I could get away with it, attempting to cover the cuts up with makeup. All of my best friends except one had moved, and school cheer fed my insecurities and sabotaged me in a way that was hard to come back from. I had one teacher in particular who seemed to have it in for me and regularly made me feel horrible (we will get to him later).

I hated school more than anything else. That remained true until the day I graduated high school. I never felt like I belonged there. Things really started to change my seventh-grade year. It felt like I couldn't catch a break. When I was noticed, it was in a negative way. I wanted to be anywhere but in school. I hated my classmates. Most of them were stuck-up assholes, and I hated being associated with them.

Everything about the school environment, I dreaded. Sitting in a classroom for forty-five minutes doing pointless activities, feeling tense and awkward every time I walked down a hallway. Eating lunch alone. Along with the stigma of having an IEP, which meant I had paraprofessionals staring me down in classrooms, I was trying so hard and wanting so bad to just be normal. Why was there no one there to notice, to help me? I felt like I was screaming, but no one could hear me.

School started to get harder for me, socially more than anything. I was known as the quiet girl by students and by teachers. I tried out for the cheerleading team at the end of sixth grade and right before the new school year started, I found out I made it, which I was unbelievably excited about. That summer, we had a couple weeks of cheerleading camp, and that was the first time I ever felt intentionally excluded. I became embarrassed to be noticed by others. I believe the other cheerleaders had an advantage because many were already friends, and being in an extracurricular activity made their friendships as a group closer.

I thought I had one girl on my side, as we were just starting to become friends when we tried out together at the end of sixth grade. She immediately changed when we made the cheer team and she became a part of the popular group— one of them. She simply ghosted me, not able to come over anymore, and didn't make conversation with me at practices. It would have been socially uncool to befriend me. I could not find my way in. Attempting to communicate with the popular crowd is difficult enough as a newcomer to the group, but when you were already seen as different, the quiet one, it was not going to happen. My social anxiety grew exponentially. I knew then, the school cheer thing was not going to be a good thing for me.

I enjoyed the actual cheerleading part. And having the whole school to ourselves for a period of time was fun as well. All of the girls were in their self-made groups, and I was always off to the side, trying to figure out my place within the team. There were a few girls I began to slowly engage with, but that engagement was merely for show. As we began practicing for the upcoming football season, I noticed how they would size me up, including the coach. I could feel my skin crawl and knew I wouldn't measure up. This was reinforced by all.

How could this be? I had been on a competitive cheer team that had won many competitions. I could do it when I was anonymous, but the social aspect of the sport ruined it. There is a reason cheerleaders have a certain reputation—I lived it firsthand.

Girls bully differently than boys, I have realized. Girls are the excluders, the "let's talk about you behind your back" type of bullying, while boys physically torment you; they take the tough-guy approach. I was rarely bullied by boys, but I definitely was bullied by girls. And let me tell you this: it is almost more painful than being thrown into a school locker. Throughout the practices, my coach almost made it a point to have it known that I was not good enough to be on that team.

We had to figure out who was going to be the "best" flyer to perform a stunt, a scorpion. They call it that because it kind of looks like one, with its tail curling up near its head. We all took turns doing it to see who could do it the best. Everyone did it okay, but they weren't great. Emily's was the best out of all of them, and then it was my turn. As I began, I was looking at them to see what their facial expressions were like, and everyone kind of stopped and looked at each other. They knew I was better but did not want me to be the flyer in the stunt.

There was a giant pause until Emily herself finally said, "Murphy's is actually pretty good; she should be in the stunt." I am very small and had worked hard on my flexibility, which is the key to being a flyer. I looked at her, smiling, as if I was saying, "Thank you." Quite a few of the girls looked at her like she was crazy, then the coach finally stepped in and said, "Murphy, yours is good, but we want Emily to fly this time."

I was only a flyer in two stunts that entire season. Emily always got to be one of the flyers. One regret that I have is not speaking up for myself at that moment. I just could not speak up for myself. It wasn't a safe environment—modeled daily by the adult in charge. I will always wonder if the cheer coach had had more compassion and more skill at working with kids who were different, if my path would have been different. Would things have turned out more positively? I can't say they would have in the overall scheme, but I know if the coach had cared about all kids and made the same effort to build a relationship with me as she did with her clear favorites, the shift that it would have caused inside me would have been huge.

Finding the courage to stand up for yourself is the biggest advice I would give to anybody. It is a valuable skill that can be carried with you throughout life. If I were to do anything differently, it would be to stand up for myself more, especially in school. The worst thing that would have happened was my classmates would have looked at me as if I was an alien had I uttered a word. And my coach would have stood there in disbelief, attempting to find anything supporting her reasoning as to why I could not fly in the sequence. If I had spoken up, I might have opened her eyes to the fact that there was no logical reason for her decision besides it being a popularity contest. Skill level apparently did not matter in this case.

It never hurts to stand up for yourself and those around you. Try it; it could open people's eyes a little bit and give them a more accurate perception of the situation.

When you are in a situation that you can't really get out of, you just deal with it as if nothing is wrong and you become almost detached from what is going on around you because, what else can you do? Looking back, that seemed to be the running theme throughout my whole seventh-grade year, partially because I was still only twelve years old and didn't fully understand what was happening, even if it was clear to everyone else around me.

When I start something, I am not one to give up easily, and it is hard to convince me otherwise, even if the scenario in my head did not turn out like I had planned. Cheer was one example.

The thing was, I knew I was good at cheerleading. I had better technique than most of the girls there, but no one else really believed in me. Why? Because I wasn't like them. I wasn't popular, therefore, obviously, I could not live up to what was expected of me. I was looked down upon for my way of being, which in turn made me pull back from the team. I didn't cry very often—at this point, I had only cried a handful of times in my life. Seems strange, but it was how I held myself together. I didn't let myself break down. After practice, I started crying and told my mom how things were going with school cheer. She was furious at the reaction from my coach. My mom called my coach to attempt to let her know more about me and to suggest some good ways to handle the situation. I didn't know at the time my mom contacted my coach, but let's just say my coach showed who she truly was. In response to knowing how I was feeling, my coach belittled me by purposely asking a few of the girls to go out in the hallway to teach me the certain technique we were learning at the time because I was slower to pick up the choreography.

She knew very well that that would just add more fuel to the fire and create more tension. If she didn't know that, then she was less aware than I already thought. When we went to another hall so the girls could "teach" me, I had never felt more self-conscious. I could see them looking at each other, mocking me with their eyes, with their secret conversations and their small smiles. There were lots of inside jokes that I knew I was the butt of. No matter how I did the moves, they had corrections to make. I had to sit there and take it. I fought the tears; I wouldn't dare cry in front of them.

Looking back, the coach should be ashamed of herself for setting that situation up. It simply reinforced what I knew—I wasn't good enough. Years later, I know that I was good enough; it was the other girls and the coach that weren't. It felt like I was always the last one to be picked no matter what we did. Whether it was just practice stunting or practicing our choreography separately in groups, I was always the last one, which was very frustrating, and the coach did not seem to care or help the situation.

I don't think she knew how, to be honest with you. She knew how to communicate with the girls who she gave the most attention, but she did not know how to react to me. She favored the other girls on the team because they were talkative and confident enough in themselves to warrant that attention. I was, and still am, an introvert by nature, and having a coach that didn't know why I was that way was hard. And having seventh- grade mean girls make it a point to indicate I was different was even harder.

After school, before the football games, we would start practicing for about forty-five minutes to get as prepared as we could. As soon as the big mob of students headed off to the buses, we began getting our uniforms and makeup on. You could most likely smell the hairspray flooding through the hallways. It was more uncomfortable for me than the practices because it was almost like I was forced to act like I enjoyed it and didn't want to crawl out of my skin. Those football game performances were not exempt from that. When I was at the games, I put all my focus on the routine itself while, every chance I got, I glanced at the scoreboard, estimating how much time was left.

During halftime, I would either sit in the stands by the girls, attempting to look like I was making conversation, or pass the time by walking around until it was time to step on the sidelines again. They, of course, did not include me in the giggling and silly conversation that they all had with each other. Nobody really noticed my incredible level of discomfort, thank God, except for my mom. She went to every game, and it was hard for her to see me like that.

The beginning of the school year started out innocently enough, with normal classroom environments and feeling somewhat like I fit in as best as I could. I feel like the moment I was diagnosed with PDD-NOS is when I noticed a huge shift within myself. I began to realize how much my school cheer team didn't give two shits if I was on that team or not. It was as if I was INVISIBLE. I was physically there, but no one recognized me, no one acknowledged me.

During practices, there was one point where we were practicing our choreography by twos while everyone else watched. There was an even number of girls on the team, so numbers weren't a problem. My name was the last name to be called because no one wanted to have me as their partner. I was always the last to be picked. I felt my coach recognized it, but she did not do anything about it; she acted as if it was acceptable for them to treat me like I was an undeserving nobody. Perhaps she didn't want to be bothered. I wish she had taken the time and had the compassion. So, from the start, I knew I was somehow, in some way, inadequate.

As the year carried on, bits and pieces of my self-esteem just fell to the floor and disappeared right as they touched solid ground. It never really came back either. As the season was coming to an end, my coach was wanting to be prepared for basketball season as far as the number of girls was concerned. I vividly remember we were all stretching in the beginning of practice, and she said, "Okay, girls, raise your hand if you want to be a part of the team for basketball season." I was the only one who did not raise her hand, sadly knowing another dream of mine was dashed.

Spend the first few minutes of class at the door or inside making connections. This is a challenging few minutes for kids like me, and it is a guaranteed anxiety-ridden start if the teacher is outside chatting with other teachers. Students need you—don't let the opportunity pass.

CHAPTER 5

All Teachers Are Not Created Equal

As soon as students got off the buses to start the school day, we all herded into the commons—really, just a fancy word for cafeteria; not all that special. I usually huddled with Emma and a few others for about ten minutes until we all dispersed to our first-hour class. From that point on, I was alone and had to take on the crowded halls by myself.

I remember one day in particular. I walked into my first hour, sat down, and observed as I always did. I decided to do something crazy. A girl who was on the cheerleading team with me did something goofy and everybody laughed, and I wanted to see what everybody would do if I did the same thing. I expected nothing but just wanted to see how they would react. No reaction. They just looked at me like I was an idiot. I wasn't really surprised, because I did it solely to get a reaction, but it just ingrained the belief that was already implanted in me. The message was: I am not good enough because I am not one of them. I am not normal.

No adults saw it happen. Before class, they were usually out by the whiteboard by our lockers, talking their own teacher gossip. If my teacher had been present, I am not sure what she would have done; I would assume nothing. She probably would just have been stunned that I actually did something that created attention towards myself and that I actually spoke willingly.

Suggestions for teachers: be present and ready when your class comes in. Those minutes uncomfortably waiting for you to come in are a vulnerable time for kids like me. This is a great time to be connected, make conversation, and get to know your students. There was also an average of three paraprofessionals in that room, which made me feel more insecure. Not that all of them were for me, obviously, but I felt like everyone knew I had an IEP simply because I was Murphy.

My second hour was health and PE class. I liked my teacher; I could tell he really cared about me as a student as well as just as a person in general, and I really appreciated that about him. I was always decent at PE and was interested in health class, so that also helped with his interest in me. My best friend Sarah was in my class before she moved, and I really enjoyed having her with me. Those were the only moments you would have heard me have to be told to stop talking. I know, surprising. I didn't have any classes with Emma, but we became really close for a while that year. Our friendship ended up growing more after Sarah moved.

Third hour, I had math assist, which was for the kids who struggled with math. *raises hand in air. * My teacher started out like all the rest, just like any other teacher until I realized how much of a target he saw me as. I seemed to be an easy target based on my lack of self-esteem and shyness, I am assuming. People who are shy are targeted easily because most people think we won't fight back, which is true in some ways. But just because we are not like every other student does not make it okay to act like we do not have feelings.

I cannot pinpoint a specific moment in time when our interactions started feeling like attacks. What would he possibly attack me for? For just being me? Because I wasn't good at math? Because I was not like everyone else? To this day, I have no idea and will never know the why. It took me a long time to come to terms with how I was treated in that class and even involved years of therapy to understand. I can only remember one or two events in which I knew in some way, why the teacher thought I deserved such hateful torment.

All I remember is actions along with words, actions that were intolerable and unwarranted. My twelve-year-old self was detached. I remember my resource teacher wrote my mom emails saying that I shut down whenever I was in the teacher's classroom. At the time, I could not make sense of it. With all the other things going on in relatively the same time frame, shutting down was the only way I knew how to deal with it. My brain brushed it off and basically said, "We'll deal with this later," because it was too much. In a way, I believed those words the teacher said were how he chose to punish me, because I already somewhat knew that I was inadequate, and I just let it happen.

In retrospect, I wish at least one of the two paraprofessionals that were in the room with me had been more of my advocate. I am pretty sure that is part of their job. I understand that they don't get paid much and they're probably bored, but kids like me need an advocate. Someone other than their parents. A teacher, a paraprofessional, someone to stand up and say, "This is wrong," when others cannot or will not. I have painfully learned that "silence is acceptance."

I never spoke about it with the paraprofessionals, but for them to not recognize something was wrong seems somewhat appalling to me because everybody else seemed to notice. And yet they never spoke a word. Having them step in would not have helped matters, I imagine, because the man's reputation as a teacher was not tainted yet. It was not until my principal and my mother got involved that the teacher would be faced with the reality head-on that he was not treating me respectfully in any way, shape, or form. He, in fact, was detrimental to my state of mind, my confidence, and was my number-two reason for cutting myself that year.

I never spoke about it with my parents or my friends, really. Actually, my friends were the first ones to speak to me about what was happening, asking me questions like, "Why is he being so mean to you?" I could never come up with an answer. The only conclusion I could come up with was I was Murphy, and that was punishment enough. I thought I deserved everything from having difficulty meeting friends to having an IEP, to my best friends moving, to the school cheer team scrutiny, to being told I was too quiet, and now, my teacher. We will call him Mr. King.

My fourth hour was science class. My teacher was nice but clearly did not understand me. I believe she tried as best as she knew how, but she kind of sent me off for the paraprofessionals to deal with instead. She would not hesitate to tell me how quiet I was, repeatedly saying it as if I didn't know. After repeatedly being told how quiet I was, it became obvious that it was not a positive thing in her mind. I knew

I was quiet; I don't need any reminding, thanks. I was not comfortable in that classroom. I felt like I could easily curl up into a ball, and no one would notice.

Mrs. Smith was always confused about how I could draw and listen at the same time. Turns out it is not all that difficult. People on the spectrum sometimes have a hard time making eye contact, especially if they feel uncomfortable. I am definitely one of them. I was listening, just not with my eyes. I understand the way some people connect with others is through eye contact, but it is not the only way. You hear with your ears, not your eyes. Eye contact can be important for engagement, but it is not always necessary because, after all, you have ears for a reason. I beg teachers to recognize this difference and appreciate it.

My language arts class, I remember the most, because I felt like I could be myself, more than any other classroom. I feel as though my teacher, Mrs. Green, already knew me without ever meeting me. I felt comfort in that because, everywhere else, I felt like nobody understood. She seemed to genuinely care despite the fact that I was not very receptive to her concern and, most of all, to her willingness to get to know me or help me. For the brief moments that I chose to speak, I felt like she actually wanted to hear what I had to say. For a while, I had a glimpse of not being invisible. I will remember her positively for this.

Mrs. Green's class was probably my favorite, not only because of her but because of the students as well. I had actual friends in that class; therefore, I felt even more comfortable, and I believe Mrs. Green recognized that. Close to the end of the first semester, we were doing a project where we had to pretend to be a character in history. As part of the project,

I was video-recorded to show the whole class. An anxiety-inducing activity. I did better than I thought I would.

At the end of our presentations, there were certain categories that you could win, and I actually won in one category, which shocked me. But I got candy whoppers out of it, so I was happy. I will never forget that Mrs. Green appreciated me, and I like to believe I was her favorite student. Positive reinforcement really does help with building self-esteem, and it is important to realize that when you are teaching anything.

Now, do you notice anything between my two classes? The teachers. I had one teacher who did not understand me and wasn't as open to getting to know me. She just focused on those who could speak in class. I also had a teacher who kind of, in an odd way, got me. She understood me for the most part, and she was willing to see me despite my quirks. Confidence is built up in a student when the teacher is not just a teacher but a mentor. I do not blame teachers for not understanding me because, sometimes, it is hard for me to understand myself. The willingness to understand or be nurturing as my language arts teacher was, was comforting. Therefore, feeling like I could perform in that class without feeling judged was freeing in a way. I was able to let my guard down (not all the way, but enough) to feel included, and shall I say, safe. Thank you, Mrs. Green.

The impact of a teacher can be felt for years and make you believe things about yourself that just aren't true! Never let someone else's negative opinion, even a teacher's, determine who you are or who you will be! I allowed this for far too long! Unfortunately, most kids don't have the development to know better, but teachers should.

CHAPTER 6

Mr. King

The day was pure torture academically, as well as just stepping foot into his classroom. Having two math classes in one day was annoying, and having Mr. King as my teacher for both of them was even more disheartening. Pretty quickly into my seventh-grade year, he perpetuated this unwavering belief that I was not good enough; I was inadequate. That it was wrong to be different.

As I have grown and matured, I have realized that forgiveness is the only way to move forward. Blaming someone for your issues or heartache is not the way to heal that wound, or to just put a Band-Aid over it. At first, I was confused and angry, trying to figure out why. Why me? Why was I the only one? Did I really deserve all that was done? I see now that, no, I did not. It was purely a flaw within Mr. King, but in turn had long-lasting effects on his students. I am not to blame. Is he to blame? Not necessarily. He could have done better. Absolutely! However, sometimes teachers just don't know how to do better. Like I said, prior to that, there were many events that occurred simultaneously, which played a part in the state of my mental health. His poor treatment and teaching methods were one part of it.

Forgiveness might be a stretch, but I no longer blame Mr. King. I hope someday I can get to full forgiveness; it just hasn't happened yet. I am not sure how to articulately portray this part in any depth because I do not remember. I blocked it out because, quite frankly, it was how I got through it. I remember little bits, not in any particular order, but I do remember some. Throughout the years, I have realized that I am not flawed in the ways Mr. King believed, but part of me does still carry the belief that I am different and, therefore, flawed. I want to make it clear that I am not putting all his dirty laundry out there to say, "Hey, look at what all he did, he deserves to be punished." No. Could it be construed like that? Absolutely. These are the things that are hard to talk about, but are important for every teacher, coach, or people that you look up to recognize. It could change those around you, those influenced by you.

Mr. King usually passed out the homework before each lesson so we could follow along and understand the material better, and this particular day, he did just that. I, not thinking it was that big of a deal, went ahead, not really listening to the lecture and doing the work on my own. Now, is it okay to get frustrated at a student? Sure, but leading the student to feel embarrassment or shame is not how you handle the situation, especially with twenty-four other teenagers in the room.

Mr. King walked over to me, leaned over, and asked in a very stern voice, "What do you think you're doing?!" I immediately froze in fear of what he would do. He grabbed my paper, ripped it, and wadded it up into a ball, then tossed into the trash can. "Don't ever do that again," he said in a very stern voice. While the whole class was staring at me. Let's just say I never did that again.

Keep in mind, I simply worked ahead on the page. This was actually somewhat of a victory because I actually felt that I understood the material enough to work on it on my own. It was not just his actions, but his overall demeanor. The way he spoke to me in that moment and any other was absolutely terrifying to me.

In math assist class, we usually practiced problems and concepts using the small, mirror-sized whiteboards which I always liked to doodle on, as did everyone else. While we were waiting for instructions, I was doodling because I could not help myself.

Mr. King looked me directly in the eye with the stern voice he used and asked me, "Why would you do that when I told you not to?"

I froze. "I don't know."

"You better listen to me, Murphy. Don't do it again."

Meanwhile, I was watching all the other students do the same thing. I can still hear Mr. King's chilling voice. After that moment, I was hesitant to draw on the whiteboards without the teacher's permission in other classes where we were using the same practice method. He sounded like he truly despised me for who I was, and that was what I had the main issue with. He set me apart in his eyes from all the others. He made sure I was different and modeled that others should look at me negatively. They followed suit. I was an easy target; I wasn't going to say anything—but likely, after these interactions, I would find a way to cut myself.

There was also a period of time where, whenever I answered something during a class lecture, which would usually be written on the Promethean board, he would erase it rather quickly as if he did not want anybody to see, no matter if it was correct or not. It would not have really bothered me if it was just done to me, but my failure almost always was publicly shared with the whole classroom.

These are a few scenarios, but there were many more on most days of the week. Some more blatant than others, but always there was the clear feeling of dislike. I never thought of sharing Mr. King's mean treatment with my parents. That thought never crossed my mind. I believed I was worthy of receiving such torment.

A month or so in, my mom realized what was going on. My mom and I were at a cheerleading competition where she overheard two girls who went to my school talking about how mean Mr. King was to me. They had no idea it was my mom sitting right next to them they were just talking amongst themselves. My mom asked me about it later that night, and I told her it was true. She was shocked and sad at this news.

I didn't believe it was bad enough for anybody to do anything about it. I knew something was not quite right in the way Mr. King interacted with me, but in my eyes, I was the weak one, and he had the power to do anything he wanted, being the teacher. Now I realize how warped my mentality was. Just because you are a teacher, a "higher-up" in any administration, or simply an adult, it is not okay to berate anyone that is "smaller" than you simply because you can. That is not how it works, my friends.

Pretty quickly after that, my mom began to get in touch with my principal. My mother is very persistent when it comes to anything, really, but especially when it comes to her children. Her momma bear side comes out. She was always open with me on what was happening and told me about the multiple sit-downs she had with him. I appreciated that she never left me in the dark. I was young, yes, but my mom being open with me about exactly what she was going to say and sharing a brief synopsis of the conversation afterwards made me mature in a lot of ways.

It is okay to stand up for yourself. It is okay to get your needs met. I am no longer afraid to ask for help to get my needs met because I know it will just allow me to grow to my fullest potential. It was a valuable thing for me to learn.

From those conversations with my teacher, principal, and mother, there was no resolution. There was no "Yes, Mrs. Jonas, you are right, I am so sorry" or even Mr. King just admitting to himself that he was wrong and needed to work on his demeanor towards me. It was more of a "you are wrong, I am right" kind of conversation. My principal, to my knowledge, had heard about this situation from multiple sources, so there was really no denying it. I never sat in on a meeting. I do not believe it would have been appropriate considering my age, and just the situation itself would mean more pain and confusion on my part.

Mr. King was shocked when either of them mentioned any evidence. He seemed genuinely offended. My mom said, "So if I put a tape recorder on her and record all the things you say to her and play it back, you think it would be acceptable?" He had no answer; he was just stunned that he'd had someone bold enough to confront him. He thought the confrontation was purely an attack on him. "You are attacking me, and I don't like it," he said.

Well how do you think I felt every day, Mr. King?

A source of evidence that my mom didn't tell me until about until a year or so later was one that shook me up and one that I will never forget. There was a substitute paraprofessional in the classroom for the day who was so distraught about the events that occurred between Mr. King and me that he felt the need to contact my mother. Several days after he witnessed the daily altercations with Mr. King and me, he went to my mom's school to tell her what he saw. With tears in his eyes, the paraprofessional said, "I just can't sleep at night knowing how he is treating your daughter, so I needed to come tell you."

I had no idea how bad it really was until I heard that statement from a witness that had only spent forty-five minutes in that classroom for a few days. Having my mom tell me that put in perspective for me how wrong the situation was. At that moment, I realized how desensitized I happened to be to the emotional turmoil that I spent a whole year trying to get through.

I had no other choice but to go to school every day and deal with the constant reminder that I did not belong there, along with the feeling of inadequacy that I felt not being like everybody else.

Nothing is more important than having a safe space at school. The hope is that all classrooms are safe places. Teachers' reactions, verbal and nonverbal, let each child know if that space is inviting!

CHAPTER 7

Safe Space

Beyond that, I did make two great friends who were in my language arts class, and I was extremely grateful for them. Emma and I did not have any classes together, which was a bummer, but it allowed me to establish new friendships. I became friends with two other girls who were already friends and invited me in with open arms. They made my days in school a little brighter and became some friends I could go to besides Emma. I ate lunch with them and had sleepovers and they were both quickly added to my friends list.

Having friends in class provided me with a sense of confidence that I could not fake. It was almost as if I was automatically allowed to let my guard down because I had two people who liked me more than I liked myself. Mrs. Green saw that as well. I really enjoyed my language arts class because I had two friends, but also, my teacher believed in me. She outwardly showed her confidence in me, which meant a lot because that was very rare.

Having new friendships did not make every unfortunate situation hit any less hard, nor did it improve the state of my mental health infinitely. Did it help? To some extent, yes, but I was still very much in a lot of emotional pain which I was pushing down. I began to inflict pain on myself during this time. At first, I did not see it as a way to distract myself from emotions; I was on a medication that sort of sent me over the edge, and I felt as though I needed to cut myself. Self-harm is not a suicide attempt. It is not an attention-seeking behavior, usually. I did not know why I was doing it when I first started. All I knew was that it made me feel better, and that was all that mattered at that point in time.

For a couple months, it was attention-seeking, solely for the reason of wanting people to understand how much I was hurting, without using words. Wanting somebody to step in and reach out to me. I would purposely not cover the cuts because I wanted someone to recognize the symbolism of the pain that I was too afraid to admit to anyone. I remember the first time I did it, it was in my language arts class. I will never forget. Mrs. Green and I made eye contact. She looked frightened, like, "what the fuck are you doing?" but she never said anything.

The more I did it and was exposed to the embarrassing consequences of my behavior, the more I realized that I did not want anyone to know. I felt uncomfortably exposed, and I realized nobody would let me keep hurting myself, so I kept it hidden. I did not want that sense of coping to get taken away. It calmed my anxiety and woke me up from the depression that was engulfing me. Hurting myself made me feel more alive. Something that I regret is not allowing people to help me, and any teacher who was willing to help me, I rejected. Not because I was a brat, but because I was fearful and embarrassed of myself. I thought I was not worthy of help. In reality, though, I wanted someone to help me.

Cutting myself was my form of coping. For a long time, it was a way to distract, a way to punish myself for not being who I thought I should be. Being the quiet, shy girl was not acceptable. My self-esteem became worse when my math teacher was always talking down to me, which just fed the behavior.

One day I got called into the school counselor's office because a teacher saw cuts on my arm. I remember denying it, saying I got scratched by a tree. I don't think she bought it. I asked her who told her, and she obviously could not provide me with a name, so I had my guesses. Afterwards, the teacher called my mom, so I asked my mom who sent me. She told me it was Mr. King. I was shocked, stunned, and truthfully, angry that he felt so concerned that he needed to get the counselor involved when he was doing what he was doing. He never thought he played a part in my inner self-hatred, but he did. Very much so.

Despite that area of my life, I continued my love of competitive cheer at Cheer Fusion, and cheerleading was my sport. Starting in my cheer journey, I began on a level-one team for another year, which fed my soul. That gym saved my life in a way. If I hadn't had that gym to run to four days a week, I don't know what I would have done. I believe I would have been in a very dark place without it. The relationship I had with my coaches and with my teammates was everything that I craved. The unity and connection that I had with other people who I had no blood relation to is what I wanted the most. That gym gave me that, and with all the other things going on in my life, the sport gave me something to live for. Knowing that I could escape for a little while was exactly what I needed.

I had two spaces that I identified as safe, where I felt as if I could talk a little louder and breathe a little smoother. I have always been close to my immediate and extended family. My home began to be my "safe space," if you will. Coming home at the end of the day was my favorite part of the day because I knew as soon as I got off that bus, I was finally safe once again. As if I was stepping outside for the first time after being in prison. My parents always comforted me in ways only they knew how, and my brothers made me laugh at the end of the day, which made me feel whole again. I began to unthaw from the numbness induced by anxiety and began to be myself.

There were many times when my teachers asked my mother if I was always this quiet.

"No, she's much more talkative at home," Mom always replied. My parents really helped me that year, even through the mother-daughter teenage fights over homework that I swore I knew how to do when I really did not. My mom was my rock. I realize that a lot of students do not have the luxury of having that safe space, which makes me even more grateful for what I came home to every day. I am extremely grateful for that. I have never fully expressed my gratitude to them in the way they deserve until now that I have taken a step back and analyzed it. I could not be more thankful for you, Mom and Dad.

To the students who feel lost and unsafe, I hear you. I was there, and finding an activity or people that make you feel safe is the best thing you can do for yourself. That safe space provides you with a purpose other than having your nose stuck in a textbook, and it distracts you for a little bit.

It provided me with a name other than the quiet, weird girl. I was a cheerleader, and I was damn proud of that title.

The end of that year was filled with confusion. I had no idea who I was or what I was doing. I was very much lost within myself, and I believe, more than anything, I needed some type of closure. Closure that I never got. As I have gotten older, I have learned how to deal with that lack. Being thirteen years old, I just was not mature enough to understand myself, let alone everything going around me. I felt as though there were many puzzle pieces missing, and I could not figure out how to put them back together.

Seventh grade really changed me in ways that I am just now beginning to comprehend.

Looking back on that time, I see a sad thirteen-year-old little girl just finding ways to make it through each school day. It makes me sad because it really changed how I viewed the public school system as a whole.

My resource teacher and I were close—closer than most of my teachers, anyway. I felt comforted by her. Even if she did not say much about what was happening, I could feel her support. She was in the room with Mr. King and me most of the time, and she could see how I was being affected by him, as well as by the other things going on in school. He was the only one who taught the students who did not fit the requirements for accelerated math. Which meant I had to take his class again in eighth grade.

One day, my resource teacher and I were talking about next year. Towards the end of our conversation, we started talking about math class. She looked me dead in the eye and said, "I am so sorry you have to deal with him again." Many years later, I can still picture her saying those words.

A teacher showing students respect is a sign of strength, not weakness!

Chapter 8

Searching to Cope

I knew I was going to be a student of Mr. King's again, which, surprisingly, I did not have any outward reaction to. Numbness was my self-protection. It was one of those things I just had to accept. Some people often forget the aftermath, the cause and effect that is inevitable. Eighth grade was the year of coping the best I could with being in that school again. I began to cope with food or lack thereof. It started out slow, then latched onto me with such force that I did not see coming.

I remember watching TV one day at the end of my seventh-grade year, sitting on the floor of my room switching through channels, trying to figure out what to watch, and stumbling upon this segment on a woman speaking about her struggle with bulimia. Something she said that I still can vividly recall is that it made her feel better. That is what I wanted more than anything; it did not preoccupy my mind fully until the summer ended and my eighth grade year began.

Upcoming eighth graders at my school were given an opportunity to become web leaders, which was a mentorship-type group for new sixth graders. I wanted to be a web leader because I wanted to help a group of kids acclimate to this new environment. Even if they were only a few years younger than me, I did not want anyone to struggle as much as I had first coming into middle school. I felt as though this was an opportunity for me to provide guidance to them, even if it was just in a small way. I remember walking into the school building to prepare for the first day of school activities for the new students, and that was when I started religiously counting my calories. It was almost like a switch went off in my brain that activated eating disorder symptoms. It happened that quickly.

I was already aware of calories, but it was as if I suddenly became conscious of the cause and effect. As a fourteen-year-old, I could not really pinpoint the reasoning behind my behavior. I just knew what it provided me in that moment; a chance to feel better. Now, looking back, it makes sense that my behaviors swelled when I began another school year.

My brain was responding with a coping mechanism that began as just an innocent trial run. From then on, it had me! Eating disorder symptoms serve a purpose that is much more complex than the preoccupation with physical appearance. The obsessive preoccupation is a distraction, a welcome one. It is easier to deal with the bubble of an eating disorder than it is to actually deal with the shit going on in your head. It was as if my brain switched and said, "Okay, we are going to deal with this by counting calories and purging."

That was what I did. At the time, I had the attitude of doing what I had to do. I didn't care if part of me knew it was wrong. There is no doubt I was fearful deep down, even if I could not articulate it. I was very wary of Mr. King for obvious reasons. I still had to have a math assist class because math concepts were like learning a foreign language to me. For a second year, I had to endure two forty-five minute classes with him as my instructor.

I enjoyed being a web leader; it was an opportunity for me to lead even if it was just eating lunch with new sixth graders once a month. It impacted them, and I am glad that I was a source of leadership for them. I still remember my web leaders from when I was in sixth grade, and I hope the students remember me as well. A few of my friends, Emma, Olivia, and Taylor, were also involved, and I enjoyed being a part of something with them.

Despite my growing friendships, I still was battling with my mental health. School was very hard for me, even if I did have friends to run to. My resource teacher from last year had too many students, which meant I had to switch teachers, which was hard for me to grasp. I still wonder, why would they switch the girl on the spectrum, notorious for having a hard time with change? As a kid, you just have to go with the adult decisions. It feels helpless, like you have no control. My resource teacher had helped me through a lot that year, and I began to have a connection with her. Having to switch was hard, and she was sad about it as well.

My new resource teacher welcomed me with open arms, which made me feel safe. Thank God! I was relieved that we got along well. In my math class, she helped everyone, but she was primarily there for my friend and me. The first day of school is usually going over the syllabus, which is always fun. Well, not really, but Mr. King showed his true colors once again by indirectly putting me down. He was giving a speech on speaking to him if you had an issue. He said not to have your parents do it for you. He glanced over as if he was speaking to me, and I felt a rush of fear and dread once again.

The next day, we had an "introduce yourself to the class" project. We had to go up in front of the class and explain things we loved, what food we liked, our name (obviously), and what our favorite sports team was. When it was my turn, I was more afraid of my own teacher judging me than I was the students, which said a lot. My resource teacher congratulated me, noticing I was uncomfortable. I was glad she knew about my social anxiety because even if we didn't really talk about it, I could tell she understood, which felt welcoming. I was glad I had people in my corner, because I do not know how I could have dealt with that had I not. The resource teacher noticed me and took action.

My mom wanted to have an IEP meeting with all of my teachers at the beginning of the school year, mainly to make sure every one of my teachers was on the same page, as well as to give them a little bit of a backstory of last year. Mr. King was in the meeting with us, so let's just say that was one of the most uncomfortable IEP meetings I ever had to sit through. I believe pretty much all of my teachers were there to help me and were aware of what was going on, which made me feel more understood going into the year.

At the time, I was embarrassed and thought that the teachers did not want to hear my shit, but I've since learned that you need to reach out in order to get your needs met, and it is okay to ask for help. I felt like I wasn't worth all of their time and attention. I really liked all of my teachers except for Mr. King, obviously. However, I was still very distant with them. It felt much safer that way. It was much easier to stay quiet than speak out because nobody expected the quiet girl to speak anyway.

There were two classes in which I felt I could be myself—the resource room and my language arts class. I really liked my teacher; he was one of multiple paraprofessionals I had

had the previous year, and I felt like he understood me on a level that no other teacher really could. He always wore a suit. When students asked him why, he always replied with the same thing, "This is more professional. I see it as a sign of respect," which I thought was interesting.

His class was my favorite because I had a lot of my friends, and I did not feel as intimidated by the other students. Perhaps it also had to do with how my teacher modeled that it was okay. He saw me and paid attention. I was not INVISIBLE in his class. My fondest memories were from my language arts classes in school, most likely because I was good at it and almost always had friends in those classes. I had confidence, which made me more comfortable to make new friends, and it helped because I knew my teachers believed in me. It made a world of difference when I knew my teachers cared and believed in me. It sounds simple, but a little respect goes a long way.

Having my teachers portray that level of understanding and confidence in turn made me have more confidence in myself. I still struggled with the intimidation of my peers, but having teachers that I looked up to made that intimidation somewhat fade away. My language arts teacher always made a point to give me positive feedback, whether it be on a submitted paper or a presentation in front of the class. Again, positive reinforcement means everything to students like me. For a project, we had to make a PowerPoint about what colleges we were interested in. Why we were assigned this as a project while we were only in eighth grade, I am not totally sure, but nevertheless, it was sort of fun.

The most dreadful thing about presentations is waiting for your turn. I did pretty well with it, and as I was walking back to my chair, my teacher looked me in the eye and said, "Murphy, good job." This sounds insignificant, but it meant everything. He said it in a very genuine way, with a surprised look on his face as if he did not think I would do that well. It meant a lot that he recognized how difficult that was for me and gave me praise. It meant a lot because most teachers will not do that.

My friendships in that class also played a big part in my confidence level. There were about four of us in our little group that we formed, and more than anything, I remember the friendships I built and those who I grew even closer to. I enjoyed being with them, laughing at stupid things, and having fun. I grew closer to Emma, and that felt really good. I felt as normal as I could get in that environment, and that is always something that I will fondly remember. In middle school, I had meaningful friendships that I will never forget, and I am beyond thankful that I got to experience a clique of sorts, with my own group of friends.

Even still, school was a place where I did not feel safe. Even though I had some areas which I identified as safe, I still felt wrong in some way. As if I was not supposed to be there; I did not belong. I enjoyed being with my friends, but it was and always has been difficult to manage my insecurities in a school environment.

I never liked to speak about my autism spectrum diagnosis. I always believed it was just a part of my personality, which is not in need of diagnosing. Admitting my diagnosis to myself was not an option. I had a really hard time differentiating between low- and high-functioning autism. Technically, I knew the difference between the wide variety of the spectrum, but all I heard was *autism*. That became a shameful word, and I did not want it as an identifier for myself. Pervasive developmental disorder is not something that goes away. As you get older and are "out in the real world," it can actually be harder to navigate.

In school, you basically have a built-in friendship group. Even if you are not best friends, you still communicate to some degree, which helped me a lot personally with learning how to socialize. In other words, my friendships were not exactly the same intensity as others my same age. Socializing has never been easy for me, especially with kids my own age, because I have no idea how to start conversations without them being painfully cringeworthy. Talking in a group with kids my own age was the worst. I felt like everyone was examining me in my most vulnerable state: talking.

Mental illness always finds a way to creep in, even if you have friends to run to. Despite my friendships growing stronger, my depression was skyrocketing. I felt smaller than I ever have emotionally but somehow still wanted to be smaller, small enough to disappear into the crowded hallways. I would try to be INVISIBLE.

Eating disorders are not about weight; weight is merely a symptom of bigger issues. I began to purge (throw up my food) during lunchtime without my friends' knowledge. I didn't even know the full reason I had the urge to throw up my food. I just knew it made me feel better, and that's all I cared about. I never realized how hard it would be sitting in that math class once again. It messed with my head even if I had sort of a friend group. I was hurting, and I just needed something to hold onto. It was my comfort. My whole world started to center around my eating disorder, especially during the school day.

It was my way of coping. I began to sneak around and leave the cafeteria without asking to do my daily purge, and if I did get caught, I would try to find a proper excuse to still leave, because God forbid the food stay inside me. The feeling of emptiness is what I was striving for. I would skip classes every now and again for no particular reason and began to isolate myself more and more from everyone. I loved my friends, but it was as if my true friends were the behaviors that were slowly decaying me from the inside out.

After about two weeks, one of my friends caught on and looked at me and said, "If you leave this table and you end up dying in that bathroom, don't expect me to come to your funeral." It made me hesitate a little, but after about a couple minutes, I got up, and she once again reminded me that she would not be at my funeral. I didn't care.

After that instance and my continual secrecy, I still was able to maintain my friendships for the most part, especially with Emma. Looking back at myself during this time, the memory is extremely vivid, yet distant. It is as if I am remembering somebody else, only to be reminded that the little girl is, in fact, me. This year was monumental in a way. I, for some reason, remember more details of my fourteen-year-old existence than I do my senior year of high school. I was floating invisibly but was still holding onto a glimpse of reality. I have my friends to thank for that. It was my last year of living in an existence in which I felt like I was not completely sucked into another world with my eating disorder.

My friendships with Taylor and Olivia began to slowly dissipate. Taylor and Olivia had a falling out which then kind of left me in the middle. Both of them started to develop new friendships, and I once again recognized how easy it was for them. Navigating my friendship circle has always been difficult for me to identify, especially as I have gotten older.

It is normal to branch out into new areas of friendships with other people, but that never turned out to be the case for me. You may wonder if this has anything to do with teaching. In a way, it does. Teachers are not destined to solely teach in the confines of a classroom. It is important to recognize and think about a teacher's impact in all aspects of the school day. How many of you teachers have recognized students who are not doing well in school? Socially? Emotionally? Really learning to recognize their personality and the way in which they see the world? That is important. Possibly more important than the everyday academic lessons. Why? It builds trust and understanding.

A baseline of understanding and open dialogue can be helpful, not only for academic purposes but in every possible way. I have had this understanding with some of my teachers, and they were the people I felt safest around because I did not have to pretend or hide who I was out of a fear of judgment. They were just there, and that was okay; that was good enough.

I feel as though I was just going through the motions, floating invisibly. Just going through every day because I had no option. I was hurting, though. A hurt that I can't even really describe. The hatred was pointed at myself more than anyone else. I hated myself, not for any specific reason besides the fact that I had this deep-rooted self-hatred, not feeling good enough. Self-harm became my way of coping with the world more and more.

The more the self-inflicted harm occurred, the more people noticed. My resource teacher probably showed the most concern out of anyone besides my parents. One day, she and I were sitting together, working on a computer assignment. She saw the cuts on my arm, leaned over to me, and whispered, "You're too pretty to be doing that." She gestured to my arm that was healing. I was not doing it as a fashion statement. I looked at her for a few seconds, not saying a word, looked back at the computer, and continued working, trying to pretend I did not hear her.

It bothered me to hear her speak about it in that way because I felt anything but pretty and was not searching for any compliments. Most people who do not understand say things like that because saying "you're too pretty" is a compliment, right? "You shouldn't be doing that because of x, y, and z." Self-harm is seen as physical pain but on the inside. There is so much more pain that nobody can really comprehend unless they do it themselves.

More than just the social and academic aspects of schooling, teachers need to become more aware of mental health. Mental health is important, and the stigma surrounding mental illnesses and mental health in general should be talked about in school because it is more prevalent than anybody realizes. Understanding the language of mental health could help teachers not only recognize it but have the tools to help their students who may be struggling.

Continuing my active lifestyle played a big part in attempting to alleviate my mental health issues. The cheer gym was a place in which I could blossom, with no judgment. Cheerleading was my sport. I began my third year cheerleading competitively, and I loved it even more than the previous year. I joined a new team, a level-two team, which I was more than thrilled about. I was more than ready for a new season, and pretty quickly, my life consisted of at least five days a week at the gym, which was my favorite place to be.

My team had more girls than I was used to, which meant more girl drama that ensued over time. It felt like a big team, mostly because there was a lot of personality among the girls, and with this new dynamic on the team, it became difficult for me to find my way in.

Even in my "safe zone," I was never good at communication with my peers. I had one teammate who I got along really well with, but even still, I felt not adequate enough. Even when cheerleading was my favorite place to be, it still did not change communication issues with my peers. Nothing did. The passion for the sport continued even long after I eventually made the decision to quit. I was able to have fun with them; I joked around like I did with my friends even in the midst of the hard-core competition season. Somewhere along the line, though, there began to be a disconnect. My team was very opinionated and talkative, and even if I felt close to them, it was hard for me to talk with them, making it harder to connect with them. To me, they felt bigger and better in comparison, which is where I now believe the disconnect began. It continued until the end of the season.

I believe my low self-esteem and confidence was showing up in my relationship with my teammates and coaches. My coach was hard on all of us, but that was only because he wanted us to succeed, and I knew that. All of a sudden, I became more sensitive and aware of the dynamic between my team and me that seemed off, as well as critiques from my coaches.

My sensitivity increased when my coaches began critiquing me, making me feel like I was less than I already felt. I had two coaches, along with the founder of the gym.

My relationship with them had always been relatively close-knit. I loved my coaches for the work they put in with all of us as a team. As the season went on, I continued to fall more in love with the sport, but my relationship with my team began to dwindle. Having PDD as well as social anxiety has always made it difficult to communicate with my peers. It is not my personality to butt in on a conversation, even in an environment I feel comfortable in.

Along with my social difficulties, I had trouble keeping up with the choreography. It was more complicated choreography than the last season. It takes me a while to learn new things, and learning new routines and choreography was no exception. Therefore, it led to frustration from my coach, which I was very aware of, which made me feel more out of place.

Cliques are formed, specifically among girls; that is just how it works. With cheerleaders, it is typically even more prevalent. It was really difficult for me to realize that my once-safe zone was beginning to slowly become a place all too familiar. A place I didn't belong.

The sport itself provided me with a purpose much more than the aspect of social interaction did. I felt like I began to hide who I was because being quiet was not acceptable. Being different was not acceptable. Cheerleading was my only acceptable form of self-expression.

My school life was not getting any easier; therefore my mental health kept declining in a way that I felt as though I needed to help myself in any way that I could. At that point in time, I could not afford to put myself in an environment which did not feed positivity. I knew in my heart that this would be my last competition season.

The gym was no longer providing the safety net that once kept my head above water. The girls were no longer a part of my social life, and I felt very disconnected from them. I felt like I became one of the weak ones. Physically weak. As if I did not know what I was doing, and therefore was not good enough in their eyes.

Somewhere around this time, I was lacking communication or rather just had a misunderstanding with a paraprofessional that was in my resource room. She was not in any of my classes but happened to be helping me with a math assignment. She was very matter-of-fact when it came to instruction. I do not recall exactly what she said, but her tone of voice I can recall very clearly. Her statement, combined with her tone of voice, sounded exactly like what Mr. King would say, and that scared me.

I do not ever remember being previously sensitive about the way the teachers spoke or regarding their mannerisms, but ever since Mr. King, that sensitivity seemed to become more evident to me. I had a competition that weekend, and my mom was considering not taking me because I was acting out in an angry way. I have learned throughout the years that I express my sadness/hurt with anger, and I was reacting very much in the way of sadness. I was angry because I did not understand.

Let me back up. I understood the paraprofessional's frustration because I was frustrated as well. I just was not able to comprehend the damn math concepts she was attempting to teach me; the frustration was on both ends. I may have been more frustrated than she was. Sometimes, even adults should take a time-out and walk away when the frustration becomes too much.

That weekend, I took part in a cheer competition, mainly because I did not want to let my team down. I loved cheerleading so much, but that weekend I did not want to be at that competition. My mom noticed that I was not acting like myself. I eventually told her what was going on, and she was understanding.

The next day, we decided to nip it in the bud. My resource teacher, the paraprofessional, my mom, and I sat down to talk about it. She got me out of language arts class to talk to them. When I heard the phone ring in class and my teacher told me to go to the resource room, I felt like my heart dropped all the way down to my feet. That was the very first time I spoke about Mr. King with anyone other than my mom, not in great detail, just enough to give context. I even got brave enough to talk to them about my eating disorder and self-harm, which was how I coped with not only the situation but pretty much everything up to that point.

By the end of the discussion, we were all on the same page, and I was glad to have all of it out on the table. Teachers are human, too; they say things they don't mean sometimes or simply lose their temper, which I understand. I was not the easiest student when it came to teaching me new concepts.

Throughout the year, I was searching for a place, an understanding place, whether that be in person or online. I could talk to people online about things I was struggling with, especially my eating disorder. Turns out I connected to a lot of sufferers who felt as alone as I did. My head was not on straight, and I was trying my best to get someone to not just listen but to do so with interest. For a while, all I wanted was some sort of friendship, and unfortunately, those I could find were struggling themselves. I became immersed in this world of sickness and mental illness, and at the time, it was okay because I found understanding within the conversations that we had.

I met this girl from Italy. I still remember her name. She seemed interested in talking with me, and that was what I was searching for. She lived in a whole other country, so obviously, continuing an actual friendship was unlikely, but that did not really matter to me. Communicating through text message was much simpler anyway.

There was one night in particular where I was feeling really low and told the girl that I was suicidal and was thinking about killing myself. Thinking about suicide is different than actually planning to follow through with the action. I did not have any intention of actually following through with those thoughts. Despite my intention, I chose to text her to receive support or validation of some sort. This ended in my mom finding out.

I was getting ready for bed. My mom came to say good night and sat down on my bed next to me. I felt more and more anxious because my mom did not know I was talking to this girl, let alone what I was telling her. "Okay, Mom. Get out, please."

My mom did not know anything about this girl; all she knew was that it was a girl that I met online. The rest of the night was filled with tears and embarrassment on my part, my mom saw the message pop up on my phone. She was obviously concerned about the intention of that message. I got my phone taken away and did not get it back for about a week or so. I decided to put this in this book because it was a big thing at the time, and it shaped the way I made the rest of my decisions from that point on. Including my decision to never get on a cheerleading mat again.

The next day at school, I was not expecting anything eventful to occur, but it turned out to be one of those days you will always remember. I was going through my normal school day and was sitting in my third-hour class when I heard the phone ring. I did not think anything of it. My teacher said, "Murphy, it's for you. Your mom is here to pick you up."

I was very confused and began asking myself, "What is she doing here?" and "Why is she picking me up?" Right when I got in the car, Mom told me that we were heading to my therapist. "Oh shit." *This is going to be interesting,* I thought.

I told the therapist all the shitty reasons why I felt suicidal, and all the normal questions therapists would ask followed. I didn't have any answers. She then believed that I was not safe, recommending that I go to the hospital to get evaluated. Based on this evaluation, I either would or would not be transferred to the mental hospital nearby. People have all sorts of different opinions on what mental hospitals are actually like, but they are not how they are in the movies, not even close.

I spent three to four days there and it was not bad, crazy enough. It was obviously not the best place to be, but in an odd way, I felt somewhat safe. People understood me there. That is the whole point, isn't it? I had self-harmed just a few days prior, and I did not feel as though I needed to hide the cuts because it turned out that most of the people in the hospital did as well. I felt comfort knowing that everyone in that place knew what I was going through, and I did not have to hide the fact that I felt bad, because I definitely did, and I was tired of hiding.

I tried to purge multiple times after meals. They did not get the memo until my last day that they should probably lock my bathroom. It didn't matter, though, because my gag reflex just stopped working. From then on, I could not purge the "normal" way. For a while after that, I blamed my school principal because the day before this occurred, I got caught sneakily running to the bathroom; the bathroom that usually had no people in it, which was all the way down the hall. Ever since then, the logical reason in my head would be to restrict because I could not purge anymore. Therefore, binging was out of the picture unless I got fat, so obviously, restricting was the only option. I was very logical, as you can see.

I was very happy to be discharged, but with that, I had a decision to make that was really hard for me, but which ultimately was one of the many reasons that led to my downfall. I was very vulnerable those first couple days after getting out, and I got to the point where I was basically forced to remove things from my life that brought me stress. Things I could control. One of them was my cheerleading life. It was over. It was an easy decision, yet also the hardest decision I've ever made. It was hard because it was pretty much my whole world for a couple years, but also because it was a few weeks before nationals. The biggest competition of the year.

I went back and forth on the decision so many times. To some people, I may seem weak for not gutting it out for about three more weeks until the season was over, but I felt like I had to quit for my own sanity. I was quickly replaced. My coaches had no choice; they brought in a girl from another team to fill in for me, and my teammates were apparently more than thrilled to see me leave.

There was a girl on my team who went to my school. She was a sixth grader and happened to be in my same gym class. That day in class, we had to run one mile in five minutes. About two minutes in, she ran up beside me. Through heavy breaths, she said, "Hey, I need to tell you something." I had a feeling she was going to tell me about something relating to me quitting the team. My assumption was correct. She told me when my cheer coach announced that I left the team, no one reacted, no one batted an eyelash, not one question as to why, but rather everyone cheered with joy. One girl screamed, "Yes!"

It was as if she was telling me to get a reaction out of me, but there was absolutely none. Not outwardly, at least. After she told me, we were all slowing down from our mile, and she quickly ran off to talk to her friends, leaving me with this new reality. I could picture my coach telling my former teammates while they were stretching at the beginning of practice. I could picture those who might have expressed their distinct enthusiasm, and it hurt, despite my expectations. I could have done without her telling me.

Losing the one passion I had was a sad and unfortunate thing that had to happen. It was my choice to quit, but the transition was hard. Cheerleading provided me with a purpose, a passion. I would be lying to you if I said I hate cheerleading; I love it and always will, and that was the hardest part of leaving because part of me knew I would never go back. Losing that sense of purpose, along with the already festering illness, catapulted me into the world of eating disorders more and more. Beginning my search for a new purpose was then my goal, and that purpose became food and the gratification of getting rid of it. I was able to purge again. Binging satisfied the void, and purging satisfied the control aspect of it all.

From this point on, I don't believe I did much besides going to school, self-harming, and binging and purging. That is not an attention-seeking statement; it is just the truth. I did hang out with Emma some, but looking back, I wish I had been with her more, establishing our friendship a bit more.

Everyone started to notice my eating patterns and obsession with calories; it was as if I was turning into somebody else; someone I did not recognize. The sole action of counting calories and purging was not a means to lose weight; actually, that did not even occur to me. It manifested itself through sadness and just wanting to be different, whether it be a physical change or a mental one. I was looking for something to fill a void, and food, or lack thereof, seemed to fill it. The rest of the year was a blur, mostly because I was numb, and just keeping my behaviors under wraps formed another layer of blurriness.

As the year was coming to a close, we began signing up for high school credits and also eighth-grade graduation. Prepping for graduating and the graduation ceremony itself was exciting. It was a special experience and one that I will never forget. The last couple days leading up to the graduation were fun. As a class, we went to All-Star Sports and rode tons of rides. It was the happiest I had felt in a while because I was in a space where I did not feel judged by my other classmates and could relax and have fun with my friends.

Graduating was a big deal. I received a necklace from my grandpa, which was special. Eighth grade was packed full of experiences, some great ones as well as some not so good ones, but you know what? I would not change anything about it. I look back, and I am sad for that little girl, but I am also very proud. Proud because I strengthened a lifelong friendship, and even though I did not believe it then, I was very strong and persevered. I was able to get through middle school.

I learned a lot from this year, but the most important lesson I want anyone to take away is this: reach out when the opportunity is given. That is something that I regret not doing. If you have teachers who you feel close with and who want to help you, you are allowed to let them in. There were many times when a few teachers offered support, and I pushed them away. You are allowed to let people in, and I wished I had listened to my own advice. You are not weak in asking for help.

I had a friend, Reagan, who began to get the cheerleading bug. Throughout the year, we had classes together, which gave us a few things in common for general conversation. One of those topics was competitive cheerleading. She knew I was involved and was thinking about joining the same gym. Don't get me wrong, I was a little jealous that she was following in my footsteps, but of course, I was happy for her. I was excited for her to get to experience the atmosphere, because that was the thing I loved the most. To be honest, I wanted someone to love it as much as I did. From what she began telling me throughout classes, she seemed to fit right in, which I was glad to hear.

About a month later, we both graduated from middle school and began our summer vacation. My average summer day consisted of either being with Emma, my family, or being a hermit in my room. That day I chose to find my inner hermit and veg out in my room all day, and then I got a call from Reagan.

Ring, Ring, Ring

I answered with an excited, "Hello?"

"Hey, Murphy. This is Reagan. I just got out of tumbling class, and Jake, one of the coaches, said some things to me about you that I think you should know."

I hesitantly replied, "Okay, what did he say?" I had a feeling I would regret my decision but let her continue.

"We were tumbling on the trampoline, and I mentioned I was friends with you. And he said, 'Really? She's slow.'"

I was standing outside my bedroom door and was silent for a few seconds, attempting to process what Reagan had just told me. I finally asked if he really said that.

"Yes," she said.

"I figured he would say something like that," I replied.

The conversation went on for about fifteen more minutes. After the call ended, I went straight upstairs to tell my mom what just happened. I was hurt, obviously, but more so because I enjoyed working with him, and from my view, that had seemed to be reciprocated. Jake was not my specific team's coach, but everyone pretty much knew everyone from tumbling and flying classes. I knew him from both because I was determined to be the best I could be and tried my hardest at learning new skills and techniques. He always seemed to like working with me and was always encouraging me to try again at the skills I needed to build. To know that was basically all a front, and realizing what he had really thought of me all this time, stung.

My mom asked me a fair question. "If she is your friend, why would she tell you something like that?"

I have never been one to gossip, at least not enough for anyone else to get involved. The truth is, I care about what people think of me, and whether that be good or bad, I want to know about it.

My mother, being the protective mom that she is, wanted to confront Jake. I am the total opposite of my mom in the way of speaking up for myself. I avoid confrontation like the plague and do not really see any reason to pick at old wounds, but despite that, I chose to follow her lead.

A couple days before, I had another semiweekly therapy appointment and told my therapist all about it. He asked me all the usual annoying therapy questions that I didn't know how to answer and then asked me how I was going to handle this confrontation. I had no clue but pretended like I had an idea. Ultimately, I had the idea of winging it.

I was beyond nervous, but knowing my mom would take the reins settled my nerves a little. My mom is a big momma bear when it comes to this kind of stuff, and you better believe she is going to tell you exactly how she feels. The drive was up the street from my house, so I had very little time to get my poised, down and dirty, telling-you-how-I- really-feel face on.

The gym was closed when we arrived, which felt weird. The gym was rarely closed in the afternoon. We walked upstairs, turned the corner into the office, and found four faces staring at me. It was a tense and difficult meeting of asking adults to take responsibility for their actions. Which was actually surprisingly difficult for them to do.

I started thinking, "Neither teachers nor coaches take responsibility for bad choices with students. Why?" Why are students not allowed to be cowards, but adults in these situations are allowed to get by with it? If you do something wrong, own it; do it for the student. They will respect you for it. If you don't, I can assure you, the student will never forget it.

While you may not be the cause of a student's anxiety, it is in your power to reduce it. Reach out, build the relationships, talk to students about normal topics. If you can't do it naturally, this is the time to fake it. Building relationships breaks down anxiety for everyone!

CHAPTER 9

How to Do High School: Warning – It Is Not for the Faint of Heart

Intimidation was one word that I would use to describe starting my freshman year of high school. I know for a fact that everyone feels this way whether they would like to admit it or not. I knew I could handle eight classes; I had done it before, but something about the new environment made me feel very intimidated. I felt like a dolphin in an ocean full of sharks.

In addition to the general atmosphere, I noticed the differences between the teachers, of course. The way they spoke, the way they interacted with students, and the way they seemed more laid-back. Most of them, anyway. My teachers reminded us often we were no longer in middle school anymore, basically meaning, get your shit together and don't be stupid. Finally, someone said it.

In every school I've been to, whether it was because of moving or transitioning schools naturally due to grade level, I have always been hyperaware of the interactions between teachers and students. For me, that has always been important. I've always been the student that teachers cannot quite figure out, but I always analyzed dialogue between teachers and students very closely. If you were to sit in a classroom with me, you would find me silent, yet in my head, I was trying to figure everyone out around me. Trying to listen to the conversations as best I could without it being too obvious that I was, in fact, eavesdropping. Analyzing the people around me has always been interesting to me, and at school, it helped me feel as if I were part of things.

Starting my freshman year, I did not have any high expectations or any bad ones for that matter. It was too new and too fresh to know exactly how I felt about this new school year with so many new experiences coming at me all at once. My mom and I went to the high school about a week before school started to walk the route to my classes to make sure I knew the lay of the land. The school was not really that big, but to me, it was like walking through a maze.

Freshman year was the year of learning and transforming. I began to speak my truth little by little and found a new passion besides stepping onto a blue mat engulfed in smoke and hairspray.

I knew my high school counselor a bit from her visit to the middle school to help us figure out our high school credits. Something I noticed right away was how she spoke. She spoke very matter-of-factly but was nice enough as far as I was concerned. She was helpful in getting me used to the atmosphere of the environment, which allowed me space to get more comfortable. She also took the time to introduce me to all my teachers, as well as the resource room. One thing she never failed to do as we stepped into classrooms was to express to them how quiet I was. "You'll really have to try hard to squeeze words out of her," she would say with her very distinct voice and jovial tone.

I understand I am quiet—that's a given—but I did not appreciate how that was the first thing she used to describe me. In a way, she was letting teachers know that I was one of the INVISIBLE kids, but it was okay. It wasn't all I was, and it felt as though they already saw me as weak without even getting the chance to know me. I got used to her ways pretty quickly, as well as her no-bullshit way of speaking.

Ever since middle school, I have always felt daunted by teachers. I was not in fear that they were too strict. The intimidation came from their overall demeanor. I was in fear that I would encounter another teacher like Mr. King. This fear was very real every year for the duration of my education. Every time I stepped in a classroom and met a new teacher, in my mind, it was almost a certainty that another "Mr. King" would show up, and I could not shake that feeling. I realized I had some healing to do in regards to my prior school experience.

My math teacher looked almost exactly like Mr. King, which logically had absolutely no correlation, but it brought up a lot of fears within me. Traumatized is a big word that should not be taken out of context, but I do believe I was traumatized by my middle school experience, and it haunts me to this day. My high school math teacher ended up being really nice and welcoming, which brought me a sigh of relief. I still had some underlying feelings that I thought would be useful for him to know. At the beginning of the year, he told us to write on a piece of paper what we would like him to know going into the year. My number-one point to discuss was the situation with my middle-school math teacher. I know, it doesn't really make sense because they were obviously two different people with different personalities, but I felt it was necessary to disclose. I was again enrolled in a math assist class that made my needs and deficits more prominent.

I expressed what I went through before in my math classes in minimal detail, but enough for him to get the picture. It gave me a sense of comfort for him to know. I liked all of my teachers that year and being in their classes, which made me more comfortable. Even though I started to feel comfortable, I still had my wall up.

Remember that IEP? Well, it followed me yet again into another school year, I was thrilled. Not really. Even if I knew deep down I needed the extra help, I had this shell of embarrassment surrounding the title. I met my resource teacher as well as the paraprofessionals, and for some reason, I tended to connect more with them than any other teachers. Maybe because they understood my academic needs or they just demonstrated good vibes. A level of understanding was always there, and I appreciated that.

There were three paraprofessionals, and I got to know them pretty well. There was one in particular who was basically in all my classes, not solely for me, but we had fun together. Fun! Imagine that? I hadn't had that in school for a long time. The first time I met her, she was on a scooter because she had broken her foot, and she was not shy about telling me all about it. She was not afraid to interact and talk to me and others, and she was not just there to help us with classroom assignments. In short, she worked at building a relationship, and it paid off.

Having paraprofessionals that I liked helped the shame that I felt go away, at least a little bit.

Three of my teachers I remember the most were my math, science, and English teachers. My science teacher, I could tell by the way he spoke to me, saw my potential. He saw past the mask I hid behind, which I liked because it takes quite a bit to do so. He also happened to be the softball coach, and one day after lunch, while I was standing beside him waiting for him to unlock his classroom door, he nonchalantly looked up and asked me if I played softball. I hesitantly said no. "Are you interested in playing?"

I was shocked at the anticipation of his voice because I had not had anyone be interested enough to ask me to be part of anything, especially my teachers. I replied, "No, not really."

"Okay, well, if you change your mind, let me know." It was amazing how seemingly interested he was in my response. To be honest, I was afraid of the social aspect of the activity. Participating in the school cheer team left me reluctant to get involved in school activities, a fear that stayed with me into high school. I was not ready to dive headfirst into another situation where I would most likely be tormented by my classmates. That wound had never completely scabbed over, and I was not prepared to have it be ripped back open. Not for a second did I feel as though I was missing out. Wait a second— that is a lie! I did know that I was missing out, but I quickly shook it off and let it go for the time being.

The class that I quickly began to love was language arts class in terms of learning to express myself. I also liked my teacher, so that helped. We were always assigned to do creative writing prompts and I soon began to build my own style in writing. In those prompts, I started to express my issues in a creative form which was not turned in to the teacher for obvious reasons. Soon after that, I began writing poetry. I did not even realize what poetry really was until I started to write it. That was when I really started to express myself.

My deepest inner demons were often the main topic of each poem, which is morbid to some, but it was very cathartic and helpful for me to creatively put words to my emotions. It was a form of self-expression that I found very useful. I wrote at least two hundred poems during my freshman and sophomore year, and it seemed, once I started, I could not stop the itch to write.

Cutting

Razor crying out for blood
Comfort, like the comfort of a baby blanket
Tears roll down her emaciated cheeks
Turning to her razor
She has no friends left

Murphy Lynne
Published in *Beyond the Sea* (poetry compilation) 2015

The itch to express my creativity in ways that did not require a verbal voice was very powerful for me. As well as writing poetry, I created my first blog, which was another platform to publicly express myself and share. My love for writing and creating has never stopped since then and has continued to be very healing. Writing has been my favorite pastime ever since.

I began to get used to the atmosphere of high school and became somewhat comfortable. However, when it came to the actual socializing part, I struggled. I have always struggled to grasp the whole social aspect of school, and even when I got used to navigating the new physical environment, I still had to navigate the people that were in it. I did have some friends that I enjoyed talking with in classes, but not really anyone that I felt a real connection with, except for Emma, of course. We had different lunchtimes, which meant I had to tackle the lunchroom by myself. Whether it was the food or the actual socialization is debatable. Honestly, it was both, but more than anything, it was the possibility of sitting by those who I did not know.

Starting a conversation with those who I didn't know was terrifying to me. First, I had to read their minds to see if they would accept me or not. Being quiet and introverted, it was hard for me to tell. I would need to take a risk. Then I needed to figure out how to either begin a conversation or find a way to fit into one. Lord help us. This did not play to my strengths.

In the beginning of the school year, I actually sat with people and communicated like a normal human being. Well, almost. It soon became more anxiety-inducing than was necessary, but my social anxiety in school was always at an all-time high so, to me, that was normal. Figuring out where I did not feel the need to flee was the difficult part.

After a while of attempting to make it work and not let my anxiety get to me, I found it was just easier to eat lunch alone. Was it sad? Absolutely! Honestly, to me, it was the safer option because of my eating disorder and the anxiety that

I felt through trying to communicate with my peers. Both my eating disorder and social anxiety were very real.

At this time, food anxiety quickly became secondary to the fear and intimidation I felt communicating with my classmates. Were my food anxieties real? Absolutely. But social anxiety and communication were always the core issue. My eating disorder acted as an easy out, a way for me to deflect anxiety towards people over the anxiety and control over food.

My school counselor kept reiterating to me the importance of broadening my friendship circle, especially in high school, with everyone sort of going separate directions, but for me, it was really difficult to comprehend, much less take action. I knew she was right, but I had no idea what she meant by "meeting new people." That meant actually talking to people, right? Crazy thought. She eventually realized I was not in the lunchroom, so naturally, she needed to investigate the situation. Why wasn't I in the cafeteria? Where was I? Why didn't I want to eat in the cafeteria with my friends?

*hahaha, friends! What a joke. *

I knew she was bound to catch me sooner or later, and I knew the questions that would come up, but secretly hoped she would just leave it alone. My answer to almost every question was, "I don't know." How else was I supposed to explain the anxiety that I felt? I couldn't. She wouldn't understand it.

At the time, I didn't understand it. The easiest way was to stick to a couple bullshit answers, followed by a reassuring smile. Almost always it ended up with her being so confused, she just ended up letting me go. If I am being honest, I was upset that I got caught, mainly because I hated that she tried hard to get me to talk to people. Sounds crazy, I know, but I was actually very content with my routine and being alone. That was what I wanted, but another part of me wished that it could just be easier to communicate with others.

I tried it for a couple days because I knew my counselor was watching me, and then snuck back into the safety of the solitude of eating or not eating (usually not eating) in the bathroom, depending on the day. My school counselor knew I was an anxious kid, but it seemed she never took that into consideration when it came to the lunchroom. She questioned me about drug use. That is the logical reason as to why a teenager is in the bathroom for long periods of time, right? It would have been easier for her to deal with a drug problem rather than a social anxiety problem, in my opinion. It would have been easier to have one designated label as to why I did the things I did. Much less frustrating for both of us as well.

She slowly stopped bringing it up as often. She probably gave up on trying to help me, realizing I am very stubborn and would not budge. I don't blame her. I wouldn't either. Eventually, I moved to the more socially accepted space of the library.

It was hard for me to explain my insecurities to anybody because I did not really know myself. All I knew was it was almost physically uncomfortable for me to sit with people who I felt forced to communicate with. I did not know how. I am pretty smart and independent, but when it comes to the simplicity of talking, it's as if my brain shuts down and programs off. Emma was shy as well but seemed to make new friends in her classes, and that made me really confused and frustrated. I was simply confused as to why it was so hard for me. Keep in mind, during this time, I refused to believe in my PDD diagnosis because there was no way in hell I would succumb to that.

That winter, I had my first high school homecoming dance that I thoroughly enjoyed. That was because I had a real friend by my side, and we had a lot of fun. Emma and I went to our first high school dance together, and it turned out by the end of the night that it would be our last. That night she dropped the official bomb, stating she was moving.

I couldn't believe it. I didn't want to believe it. She had hinted for a year or two that she might be moving because her parents are both pilots. I just had not taken her words seriously. She was moving at the end of the semester, leaving me only three months to process the fact that my best friend was moving. Another one. I felt like the universe was playing a cruel joke on me and there was nothing I could do about it, other than take it and accept it.

Those couple of months before she moved were really hard, but I knew I had to spend as much time as I could with her before she moved and do everything I could to not think about it. A couple nights before Emma and her family left, her parents and sister and a couple of her closest friends had dinner together. It was the last time I would get to spend quality time with her for a while, and coming to terms with that realization was brutal. Her parents drove me home and when I got home, I just cried and cried in my room. Emma was my last friend left, and I could not wrap my head around that. I felt like I was being smothered.

A couple days later, she moved to another city three hours away. I was used to seeing, talking, and hanging out with her whenever I wanted, and the convenience of our friendship was no longer. She was my last friend left, and I could not wrap my head around that. I had nobody left. I was really close to her family as well. They were like my second family, and I felt a sense of safety when I was with them. It was the first time in a while that I felt a sense of emptiness not only emotionally but physically as well.

For the first time in a long time, I felt truly alone. I had no one to consider a best friend that lived in close proximity. I had "friends" that I met in classes, but I say that very loosely. I did not feel connected to them to the point I could call them true friends. You learn quickly after you graduate who you communicated with simply because they were in the majority of your classes as opposed to being actual true friends.

The next four years of high school consisted of small talk between my classmates, which I did not particularly mind. I enjoyed being alone, for the most part, mainly because it was easier. It was easier to be by myself because I did not have to worry about pleasing anyone or being judged by anyone. I just had to worry about myself, and I felt at peace with that because it was easy. Did I miss talking to friends? Of course, I did. I would definitely be lying if I said I didn't, but it was too difficult and created too much thought and self-doubt in my head to even bother. I am pretty good at adapting to whatever I am faced with, and as time passed, it got easier to be alone. It was always a shadow for me in the background, but it did get easier. The hard part was, the easier it got to be alone, the more INVISIBLE I became.

I began establishing my new normal, which was going to classes, engaging in small talk, and sitting in the library during lunch. Those thirty minutes usually consisted of either writing or going through my phone, usually swiping through Tumblr. That was pretty much my routine every day besides going to a theater program that I was involved in outside of school. Of course, the goal was to also cultivate friendships, which did not go as smoothly as I hoped.

I had a role in *My Son Pinocchio*. I had other small roles, but it was relatively fun and it was something for me to get involved in besides being in the school environment. I'd always sort of thought I would be a theater kid. When I was younger, my mom would sign me up for theater camps that I enjoyed. My social anxiety was not there when I was on stage, as twisted as that sounds, and that was a nice welcome. It was almost easier to perform for people who I did not know, which is why I felt so comfortable. They did not have any biases or preconceived beliefs about me before seeing me on stage, and I really enjoyed it. Being a part of a play helped a lot. I was able to be distracted by performing a different character, therefore escaping reality, but doing it in a fun way, not a destructive one.

During Christmas break, I got a fun surprise when Emma invited me to spend four days with her. Obviously, I was all for it and so excited to see her again; it felt like forever even though it had only been about a month. Her parents have a plane and we got to fly, which was pretty cool. I felt special. I hadn't felt that way in a while. I immediately could feel myself become whole again and was immediately at peace. I felt like I could really truly be myself, other than with my own family, and it was nice.

Emma was living in a really nice rental condo, and we pretty much just picked up right where we left off as if we hadn't even been apart. Our parents always said how oddly similar we are. The way we interacted was the same, as well as the things we had in common. It is really nice to have a friend that is so similar to you that you can have no filter.

I brought in 2014 with her, and it was a fun time. The moment I had to fly back, I got sad because I knew exactly what I was going to get into when I came back. School—and that meant no friends, which meant hiding myself. I was not ready to face that again.

At that point in time, thoughts of restriction were pretty much a constant. To those who don't understand eating disorders, the best way I know how to explain them is this: The thoughts/behaviors are always there, just at different levels of frequency. Whether the symptoms are physically wreaking havoc is irrelevant in terms of understanding eating disorders. The thoughts are almost like a nonstop roller-coaster. For the duration of my disorder, including in high school, there were points where it was very active, as well as points where it was just steadily lingering in the back of my brain.

Freshman year, my disorder was there in the back of my mind, just doing its normal chatter like it always did. I can describe it as the point of the roller-coaster where it is slowing down but never stopping completely. My eating disorder appeared the most around lunchtime. Obviously but it is not the anxiety that you might think. The social aspect of the lunch environment played a huge factor in the eating disorder behaviors overpowering me. Which made me not want to associate myself with the lunchroom at all. As teachers and adults in charge, please be willing to look at the whole child and not just at the surface. Take the time to dig a little deeper.

> Be generous with compliments, even if you don't mean them at first! This draws students out and is the beginning of a relationship. When you get to know the students (especially the hard-to-get-to-know ones), you can then give genuine compliments. Don't be shy about letting them and their parents know. The return in attention and effort just might surprise you.

CHAPTER 10

A Version of Popular?

Sophomore year. I have to say it was probably the best year I had in high school. Can I say social? I know, social and myself in the same sentence is unheard of, but it's true, believe it or not. Friends are something that I was hopeful for.

My way of seeing friendship may seem somewhat odd to some who have not experienced social anxiety. I wanted friends; I've always wanted friends. Who wouldn't want friends? I simply lacked the skills to do so. It required too much effort, too much thought, and way too much anxiety; therefore it was just easier to simply let it be. This is the stuff that no one really understands. Many therapists have asked me, "Why?" I am very confused by myself as well, believe me. My answer was not always the truth.

Looking back, the reason I refused (with everything I had) to believe my diagnosis of PDD is that I was embarrassed and afraid of misunderstanding. I saw my diagnosis as admitting to weakness. Of course, I would be the last one in the room to accept being weak. Even now, I am puzzled by my own logic in regards to the whole concept of friendships and social anxiety. Trying to make someone else understand it is nearly impossible, unless they pick my brain apart, literally.

Despite my anxieties surrounding friendship, I developed some, can I almost say, friendships? Really, they were just people to chat with in class, but on a higher tier than small talk, which was an improvement. And that is all I needed— people that I enjoyed being around. One guy was new to our school. We liked to goof around in class with a friend of his as well as a few other girls. In a lot of my classes, there were people that I got along with, which made class more enjoyable. There did not seem as much pressure to be a certain way, which gave me permission to come out of my shell a little bit. I had a majority of people that I liked talking to or even just listening to in all of my classes, as well as fun teachers. I preferred teachers that had fun teaching and who didn't just teach like robots. Doesn't everybody, though? Having a group of like-minded students in combination with good teachers made a world of difference for me.

Since having a couple friends in some of my classes, I became comfortable eating with them.

gasp

I know, I even shocked myself. For the first time in a while, I felt like I belonged somewhere. In a friend group setting, at least. This was by far the best year of high school. In my resource room, we got a new teacher; we'll call her Mrs. Robbins. A couple of her daughters were students in the same school where my mom was a principal, so she knew my name. I got along with her right away. It made being in class so much more inviting.

After my mom learned about my declining the invitation to play softball, she wanted me to be involved in an extracurricular activity. Whether it be physical or not, she just wanted me to get involved in something. I chose cross-country. I chose it mainly because my school counselor mentioned they were a welcoming and accepting group of kids, which had me intrigued. I also did not want to hear my school counselor ask a million and one questions if I hesitated. I had to at least try it. So, I went for it, with my walls up.

I also wanted to get better at running; that was my main motivation. You did not have to try out, I don't believe; it did not really matter if we did, because I did not last long enough to know. During the summer, we trained for the upcoming season. It consisted of early morning runs which were about five miles long, combined with some conditioning. I enjoyed running for the most part. I liked to test my limits and stamina and wanted to improve my time and improve the little stamina that I had.

Like everything I did that had to do with my peers, I compared myself to my teammates. It was hard for me to keep up, and I was embarrassed when I had to do the walk of shame—in the running world, of course. Last one to walk up after the run.

In my eating-disorder-warped mind, that embarrassment went to a whole other level.

I felt weak by not being where my peers were, and that weakness and shame felt very uncomfortable and scary. Looking back, I realize that most of my teammates had been running for a long time; therefore their stamina was at a greater level. In the moment, I realized that fact, but my embarrassment was more related to the people. I assumed that they thought I was weak and not good enough. They also had friends within the group from previous seasons, and I did not. They ran in groups, talking. If I had talked, I would have sounded like a dying horse gasping for air. After about a week or two of summer conditioning, I chose not to be on the team.

My coaches were really encouraging and nice, which helped me feel a little better, but I still felt inadequate. I do believe cross-country is a great sport to be involved in, even if my experience did not last long at all. My mom was proud that I at least gave it a shot for a little while, and I was proud that I did as well. It turns out my mom did not want to push me into an unnecessary uncomfortable position, which is why she did not mind me quitting cross-country.

As I am reading my words, I am realizing how in my head I was in regards to what my teammates thought of me. In reality, they probably did not even care to the extent that I created in my mind. Honestly, they didn't give a shit whether I was at my best or not. They were absorbed in what they were doing.

My advice to anyone who notices a student or their own anxiety getting the best of them and having it dominate their brain space is to say this: Nothing is as bad as you make it out to be in your head. My thoughts were totally perceived ideas that had absolutely no evidence surrounding them. If you want to do something, go for it, and do not let your mind take over into negative thinking. You will offer yourself so many more opportunities if you just get out of your own head and keep going. I wish I had known this lesson then. My perceptions and anxieties stopped me more often than not.

Other than my usual insecurities, I felt content with the school environment I was in, at least the best I could. Having friends and people to socialize with was the catalyst for that, as well as having teachers that I felt a connection with. I had great teachers that year. Every year, I had at least a few teachers whose classes I enjoyed being in and who made school days less daunting. In my English class, I was very expressive with my writing, often not realizing what I had written until I actually took a step back to read the assignment.

When I write, whether it be a journal entry or a school assignment, if it's an interesting topic, I tend to get lost in it. The creativity and rawness that I experience with writing is something that never gets old, and I believe my teacher recognized this through my writing assignments. During parent-teacher conferences, my English teacher told my mom I was an amazing writer and had talent, which gave me an insane amount of confidence. He was one of my teachers who saw past my walls and seemed to actually be interested in what I had to say through my writing. Most teachers just brush kids like me off and do not see through our walls we build up so high. Thank you to the teachers who decide to beat those walls down and take the time to get to know us. It means a lot. I know it is more work.

Ironically, when my mom shared with my English teacher that he was one of my favorite teachers, he was genuinely surprised. He had no idea that I had any positive feelings toward him. I wasn't the type to show it. I had a bit of a problem with resting bitch face. My mom shared with him that I felt this way because he said hello to me while making intentional eye contact every single day. He noticed me! I wasn't INVISIBLE. He seemed surprised and had no idea his acknowledgment meant anything—it was just what he did. To me, he cared more than the other teachers who were too busy talking to the easy students, preparing their materials, not taking the time to say more than a simple hello.

It was a fun class. He made it entertaining, as did the friends I had and, drum roll, please ... a boyfriend. Yes, I know, the shy girl had a boyfriend in high school. What do you know? For about four months. He was seen as a nerd, and we got made fun of for being together. Whether they were making fun of him or me, I don't know, but there are always those people who think they're better than everybody else and believe me, throughout that time, I recognized plenty of them.

Those judgmental people made me more insecure about receiving help from paraprofessionals. I had two friends who did not feel ashamed of the thought of going to the resource room to gain a better understanding of an assignment. I had a hard time understanding how they could just easily do this without major self-criticism and embarrassment of what the other students in the classroom thought of them. The reality was they just did not care as much as I did, and that is the truth. I cared a lot about what my classmates thought because I did not want to feel any more like an outcast than I already felt. The only time I knew seeking out help would be best was when I needed a quiet space during tests.

As awful as it sounds, I often felt as if I was superior to my other resource friends for a reason that was purely out of my own insecurities and the "rules" I put on myself.

I would secretly pride myself on the fact that I was not associated with that "weakness." It was a ridiculous thought.

Certain paraprofessionals respected my decision, while others did not read between the lines and gave me a look, asking, "Are you sure you don't want to come?" Thank you, but no thank you. What I really thought in my head was "get the hell out of my face and leave me alone." It was also the way in which they approached me. If you approached me with any hint of control, I would get upset and retaliate. Do not tell me what to do! A little like when I was little and would yell, "All by my yelf!"

There were paraprofessionals who actually made me feel like a "normal" student, while others just bombarded me with questions as if they did not believe me. Every once in a while, it was needed, but doing assignments with a paraprofessional breathing down your neck and treating you as if you have little ability to absorb academic tasks is the opposite of helpful. In those moments, it became unhelpful and just plain annoying. That bothered me more than I could put into words. It bothered me even more because, for once, I was seen as "cool" by my friends and my boyfriend, and I would be damned if that perception was taken away—especially by something that was not necessary.

I refused to let anyone help me because I wanted to be independent. I had my independence going for me, and that is a trait that has always stayed with me. I can figure things out alone, even if it takes me a little longer.

My brother was heading into his seventh-grade year. I was scared for him more than might have been warranted, but since he is my brother, I felt the need to be the protective older sister. Now, I had to keep in mind that he has the polar opposite personality of me. He is the outgoing one, the kind of outgoing where he can participate in more than one event and still be itching to go out with his friends. Astounding. Whereas I could be at home for a whole weekend and feel content. His outgoing nature eased my mind a little, but I was still concerned for him. My mom reassured me that he would not be assigned to Mr. King as a teacher, which brought me a sigh of relief. The catch was, Mr. King was still going to be my brother's football coach, which terrified me.

My brother has played football since third grade, and it quickly became his passion, so naturally, he wanted to be on the middle-school football team. My mom also reminded me that everyone has different experiences despite their personalities, whether they are the same or different. It was difficult for me to expect anything more than what I got because that is all the experience I could base anything off. In the end, by no surprise, my brother ended up completely fine. In fact, I was a little jealous.

> Don't just pay attention to the superstars. There might be a student who simply is too afraid to ask for help. Be the one to ask first!

Chapter 11

InVISIBLE

Junior year was an interesting year, shall I say. It was rather eventful, while at the same time somewhat lonely. It wasn't like sophomore year. Not only because of the lack of friendship. The loneliness was not a physical feeling but rather an emotional one. I tried to hide my eating disorder the best I could; believe me, I tried my very hardest. We'll save more of that for later. My restricting, and the thoughts associated with it always swelled to a whole other level when I started school again. So, as usual, it took up the majority of my brain space when I was supposed to be having fun. During the summers, the anxiety was present but was not as driven by self-hatred and insecurity. School was my biggest trigger by far, and that is a sad fact, considering I spent most of my time there.

I was told by my teachers and those who had been through high school that junior year was the best year in high school. Whenever I heard someone tell me excitedly, "You're a junior! That was my favorite/best year. You are going to love it!" I never understood their excitement. I never understood the hype, and I did not experience the so-called "amazingness" of the magical eleventh-grade year. It was not awful, but the words "amazing" and "favorite" do not come to mind.

With three years in the same building under my belt, I felt like I knew what I was getting myself into, and that alone gave me a small piece of confidence. Having that sense of knowing made me more comfortable. My anxiety and my eating disorder went hand in hand. They fed off each other really well, so I guess it makes sense why I was a total wreck. It is often hard to tell which one came first, the chicken or the egg, or which one fed off which. This time, I believe it was anxiety.

Junior year felt odd to me. I was no longer the baby of the school, and that was somewhat intimidating. In the grand scheme of things, no one gave a shit, and I knew that, but I couldn't help but feel like I had to get my shit together.

In the beginning, my anxiety was mostly surrounding the concepts of having friends or simply attempting to talk to people. I had no idea how to do so. I mean, I knew the basics like everyone does. The whole, "Hi, how are you?" "I'm good, how are you?" The socially acceptable answer is always "good." Besides that, bringing up conversation is not something I always knew how to do. I was craving social interaction, but I had no idea how to satisfy that need, if that makes sense.

I had broken up with my boyfriend, so that was no longer an avenue for socialization. I sort of knew that the friendships I had made last school year would float away over the summertime. Mainly, I couldn't picture us hanging out outside of school, and I got the vibe that they were solely acquaintances. This was a good thing because they were people to be with during school, which made the school day more comfortable for me. When another school year began, we talked, but not nearly as often because of different class schedules and the dynamics of those classes. As the year went on, those "friendships" dwindled pretty quickly.

I did grow friendships; I say *grow* with a minimal grain of salt with some people I had known since late elementary school. We all had IEPs, but that was the only thing we had in common. However, it brought us together for the most part. I had a hard time relating to them in any way other. They were nice enough, and they were people that I could talk to, even if the topics were redundant. I was being social (somewhat) and they liked me, so why would I reject that?

Speaking of IEPS, the resource room took a little bit of a twist. The two paraprofessionals that we had moved to a different classroom; therefore we needed someone to take their place. We got two new paraprofessionals and they seemed nice, normal, and poised. They both were personable, which I really liked, and I quickly began to feel more comfortable with reaching out for help, school-related and beyond.

Within a week of being back at school, along with my ongoing fear surrounding every aspect of school, it did not take long for the inevitable constant anxiety to begin. I began having anxiety attacks almost every day, and it was the kind of anxiety that you can't hide even if you really want to. When I get really anxious, I get this red blotchy-looking rash on my neck and chest. Throughout this bout of severe anxiety, I was really glad that I had the teachers that I did. My resource teacher really helped me and did not make me feel ashamed for being so anxious; she just wanted to help. It turns out all I needed was new medication and it brought down my anxiety significantly, even though it was still just below the surface.

The resource room has always identified as a safe space for me. I knew if anything went wrong, I could go in there and be okay, which helped with my anxiety as well. I did not feel judged; I felt normal, which was an inviting feeling. The classrooms where I felt safe had to do with who the teachers were and how well I got along with my peers in that room. I had a few classes I liked. Not very many, but you could tell which class I liked depending on if I actually spoke in it.

My algebra teacher, I liked a lot. She was one of those few teachers who seemed to enjoy communicating with the shy and "unusual" ones, rather than the popular kids. Inside the classroom, at least. I admired and appreciated her for that. She was the cheerleading coach, and I had hesitations about whether I would get along with her for that reason, but she ended up being one of my favorite teachers. She was not just teaching to teach; she was also initiating relationships with her students, which I believe is a key trait that should be practiced by every teacher. She was the main person who set the stage for how I would feel and be accepted. She did not make me feel like an outcast. She treated me like any other student, which made me feel a sense of safety.

Feeling that safety inside the classroom was what I craved, and actually receiving that felt amazing. Physical safety is key, but receiving that emotional safety is equally important. Creating that safe space is important for students like me. Most likely they only have a few classes where they feel safe, and having one or two classes that I could call my "base" was what I needed.

Math, like three-fourths of the planet, I struggled to comprehend. I will never understand people who like math. Math concepts were like attempting to learn a foreign language. I could not understand it, no matter how many times it was taught to me. My teacher was really patient, which lessened my feelings of being a burden for not understanding those confusing concepts. Somehow I passed the class, barely, but nonetheless passed. Thank God. I have my teacher to thank for that.

Feeling safety in certain classes was key for me, and I was beyond grateful for it. Yet I was still longing to be a part of something, whether it be a group of kids or an extracurricular activity. I wanted that feeling of connectedness, but I was afraid, afraid of it not working out or of having students judge me because that is what I was accustomed to. I was not sure if I was ready to step into an environment different from all that I had known previously.

To some people, it is difficult to understand why you have such a craving for something but also are so scared of the result that you find it easier not to touch it at all. It's confusing to me sometimes as well. It is frustrating when my social anxiety and PDD get in the way of something I want to do. Perseverance is the only thing that can get us through.

My English teacher was a part of the thespian club. To all the people who do not speak theater, a thespian is basically what you call people or things relating to the theater world. Establishing new friendships was not successful for me unless I was in a somewhat forced environment. I really wanted to try it, despite my fears. Putting myself in that environment, I knew, would be a likely place to make friends because it put students together with a common goal.

My school counselor wanted me to get into something and surprisingly, I was not opposed to the idea but was still wary about it for obvious reasons. She thought it would be a nice way to dip my toes in, which I agreed. One day, when the bell rang and everyone was scattering to get to their next class, my teacher had her eye on me and said, "Murphy, come here a second."

Like every student, I immediately panicked at the thought of what she wanted because she never really talked to me. Most of the discussions that started with that sentence involved one of two things. You were either in trouble, or you were politely being told to get it together in regards to grades. I predicted the latter.

I walked up to her and my teacher told me, "If you are looking for something to do, the theater is a good place to be. You should go in there during lunch and talk to some of the kids."

I was surprised that she was talking to me about this. It didn't occur to me that my counselor had planted the seed. She went on, "Some of the kids eat lunch in the theater room and are really nice. I am just leaving that option open for you."

I thought about it for a couple seconds. "Yeah, thanks, I might try it out." I walked out of the classroom feeling somewhat excited to have an opportunity to be in a group of people who might be like me. Yet also kind of embarrassed because her referencing lunch made me think that she knew I was alone during that time. The theater seemed like a comfortable, safe space to develop new friendships and also learn some things regarding theater. I was willing to get out of my comfort zone slowly.

I took the advice from my teacher and signed up to be a part of the fall play. I signed up to be behind the scenes because Lord knows I would not be a part of the onstage cast. On the sign-up sheet declaring your interest, there were options you could choose from, depending on if you wanted to be the center of attention or not. I, of course, was planning on being partially nonexistent. You had to choose three crew departments, just in case. The three I picked were set design, props, and costumes. Did I know a thing about any of them? Nope. They sounded interesting enough, though.

The beginning of my theater experience was brand-new to me, in the school environment anyway. About a week later, I was anxiously waiting at my computer to see if I got in, and I did! Costumes. I had not stitched one thing besides my awful attempt at making a pillow in a consumer science class in middle school. That was comical.

When everyone knew all their roles, we all got together to introduce ourselves, which consisted of saying our names and what crew we were in. It seemed a little intimidating, but like everything else, I was up for the challenge. In hindsight, this was a missed opportunity—I should have stood up and shared that I didn't have the first idea of how to sew.

I had no idea where to begin to even start the costume-making process. Of course, with my luck, this play required multiple costume changes. My theater teacher was busy making sure the actors and actresses knew what they were doing while periodically checking in on the backstage crew. Since she was mainly in charge of the people who were on stage, there were two crew heads that were "in charge" of the rest of us. They were hand-picked students to maintain the backstage crews, who were nice kids, but bear in mind were also teenagers.

My crew had been in theater for a while, which had its advantages. I was able to learn from them. I believe they thought I knew what I was doing since I got chosen for the most complicated crew, or so it seemed. Now, it was nice of them to think I was capable of more, but they pretty quickly realized I had no idea. At first we only had a couple nights after school where we worked on the beginning stages of the costumes. It actually started pretty well and was collaborative for a short time period.

I took the advice of my English teacher and began going into the theater classroom for lunch. I felt pretty normal being in there; it was easy to talk and get a word in, even if I hardly knew them. I am quiet by nature; I like to listen and observe, which I did the first couple days, and then I got around to actually talking to the students and it was fun. It was kind of like a secret room that nobody really knew about except for the theater kids, which was cool. I consistently went in there for a couple weeks, and then I started to become a bit reclusive, for no other reason than I felt like I was getting too comfortable and that scared me a little bit. I did not want to get too close to them in fear of being turned down.

Like I said previously, the crew heads were nice for the most part. They seemed to know what they were doing, considering all direction came from the teacher. The student leadership quickly became frustrated and irritated that I didn't know what I was doing. I felt uncomfortable. Every student in the school was super intimidating to me, even the nice theater kids, and it made it difficult to speak my truth. I always felt a couple steps below them. You would think having someone in the group who does not know what they were doing would force a spark or connection. That did not really happen. In a perfect world, a scenario like that would happen, but unfortunately, we do not live in such a world.

I was embarrassed and ashamed because I felt like an outcast and they did not seem approachable, at least not the kind where I could ask them questions. There are many ins and outs to this experience, and the consensus of it was it was not my thing.

Like any social activity, there are cliques and groups that are formed; theater is not exempt from that. No matter how seemingly nice the atmosphere is. My lack of knowledge of making costumes from scratch and my issues with connecting with people set up another social disaster. It got around fast that I was not doing my part, or so it seemed. It could have been slightly true. Was I willing to learn? Not when I felt this uncomfortable.

Being thrown into something that required actual skill to create costumes and just being expected to know because everybody else knew was hard, and left me feeling out of place from the beginning. Could my teacher easily recognize my confusion? Maybe. It was as if she put the pressure on the other girls to teach me, and I was not about to step on their toes. It felt like middle school cheer all over again. It was sort of a shit show from the beginning. It was an experience, yes, but it would have been an even more valuable one if I had more understanding and one-on-one time with the teacher actually teaching me. Imagine that.

After a couple months of preparation, the dreaded tech week came, and it was the most brutal week for me. It consisted of having thirty minutes of free time after school and staying until 10 p.m. until production day. They were very long days, which led everyone to be stressed and exhausted. That long week, we had some parents volunteer to provide dinner. It was even worse than any of the other nights because I was forced to at least attempt to socialize with people. It had begun—the sideways glances and whispers among the other girls, never including me. I knew this scene.

Every night leading up to the production, we all went to the auditorium to have our annual nightly wrap-up meeting to see how things had progressed and what we needed to work on. I was uncomfortably sitting next to my crew, trying to not pay attention to where I was because I did not want to be anywhere near them. At one point, I looked over and saw two of the girls whispering about me. I could tell because they were looking directly at me, and that was the point where I broke.

When we finally got to leave at 10 p.m., I walked to my car and instantly lost it. I was crying so hard I could barely see the road, and when I got home, as hard as I tried, I could not keep it to myself. I let my mom know about the way they were talking about me and how they were indirectly treating me.

The moment she saw how hurt and upset I was, my moms motherly instincts kicked in. She and let her know what was going on, even though she should know what was happening, being the teacher, correct? Not always, apparently. It was the shameful realization once again, I did not fit in. I was in English class, and my teacher told me that Mrs. Shaw wanted to see me. I immediately knew my mom had something to do with it, which made me dread going to Mrs. Shaw's classroom more. I walked in with her sitting on one of the multiple couches she had in that room.

"Hey, Murphy, come have a seat," she said as I walked over towards her, trying not to seem obvious with my hesitance. I remember thinking, "Where was this conversation a month ago when I really needed some adult support?" She started off with the phone call she had received from my mom, which I had no idea about—embarrassing. I did not really give her much except for the bare minimum, because part of me knew nothing would change. There were several reasons I didn't really take part.

1. I hate confrontation. (I am not good at it.)
2. It was too late in the game.
3. If she had just taken the time to pay attention to the situation early on, maybe this could be avoided.

She then taught me to stitch, as if that mattered at this point. She asked me if I wanted to talk about anything else and I said no and left, feeling misunderstood and frustrated. A feeling that was all too familiar from teachers in my life.

In the midst of attempting to find myself a social circle, it was still difficult to be understood by my school counselor. It seemed as if she was only communicating with me about my lack of compliance with socializing in the lunchroom. She was more comfortable with the popular kids, I am guessing because they were easier to talk to. She liked to assume things about me, and that seemed to be the case ever since she met me. It was as if every time I sat in her office, she was silently analyzing me. Just like everyone else, she identified me as the shy and quiet one.

I didn't feel she handled my situation in the correct way and felt like she never took the time to talk it out with me. Rather, she just wanted a magic answer to say, "Yes, finally, I figured you out!" Turns out, I am more complicated than that. I feel like I am a really complicated Rubik's cube; you think you have figured out one side only to find three other sides to solve. I guess I like to keep people on their toes.

I believe the counselor tried in all the ways she knew how. She just did not understand. Even I have a hard time explaining my PDD and social anxiety, simply because I do not have the words. For people who do not understand, it makes it even harder to explain. I could see that she was more experienced at the academic part of being a school counselor rather than the emotional side. It was hard for her, I would imagine, given that I did not want to disclose any information to her. I knew her answers would not be helpful, and my words would easily be misunderstood. That has been my experience. Other than my emotional needs, she was nice to me—relatively, anyway—and that was enough.

It was okay because high school was almost over! I could do it. I would repeat this mantra to myself.

> Each year there are students who are terrified to come
> back. Be aware of them. Make a plan to be inviting, and
> understand anxiety is real and impactful at times of change.

CHAPTER 12

The Final Countdown

Senior year. Finally, my last year of dealing with a school environment ever again. Praise Jesus. Unfortunately, there was the part where you had to get all of your credits in order to graduate. Damn. I guess we have to go over the part before graduation. Let's start with the summer before senior year. During the summer, my mind was somewhat clearer. There was less anxiety; therefore you would think that eating disorder behaviors and thoughts would be less. Unfortunately, that is not how it went. It was another difficult summer taming the need to be smaller, to have control. I believe I was trying to tame the loneliness that I felt in regards to having very few in-person friendships.

I had an online friend which, at the time, was great, but there is something about having friends that live close by that makes you feel less lonely. The rest of the year consisted of weekly therapy sessions and the off-and-on friendship I had with the online friend.

Despite that, I was terrified to begin the school year, more than usual, I would say. A couple days before school began, we decided to have a family movie day as in going to the actual theater, which was a rarity for all of us to attend. On this rare occasion, my dad wanted to come see the movie with us, so we all went. Before the movie, we decided to go to dinner. With school approaching fast, it was only fitting for it to become a topic of discussion. The conversation was geared towards my brother first, who was going into freshman year. The first year of high school is a big deal, and he was excited. He was ecstatic about starting football, and he seemed pretty confident going into the year which, again, brought me a sigh of relief.

I knew I was just waiting in line to be asked the same question. The emotion that came through shocked even me, and my parents even more so. They expected the normal response I always gave: "Thank God, I'm finally almost out of there." All of a sudden, I found myself crying almost uncontrollably, which I never do, especially around my parents.

"The thought of being in a classroom again makes me want to die," I said. Looking up through tears, I saw shock and worry on their faces. My mom lovingly asked me what we could do to make it better and, in reality, there was nothing that could be done except magically skipping senior year and still being eligible to receive my diploma. I would then be done with school forever. I would have killed for that to be the case.

I'm not a crier; I'm not particularly sensitive in that way. When I do let my guard down, it is usually brought on by a topic that is painful. I am a pretty logical person, and I knew nothing could be fixed. There was nothing that could be done except to totally exempt it from my everyday world. I hated walking into that building day after day, expecting nothing besides what I knew, and all I knew was that it hurt like a son of a bitch. I knew what to expect, and it scared me to death. Something about this year scared the shit out of me, more so than any of the others. Most likely because it was my last year. I was leaving at the end of the year and did not have any plan at all except for getting my ass across the stage with diploma in hand.

I remember walking up to the school and seeing our new principal shaking hands with students as we were walking into the building. Walking in to see a few teachers handing out hard-copy schedules, I stood in line, periodically glancing down at my phone, pretending I was actually scrolling through social media. In actuality, I was just scrolling mindlessly, hoping that Heather would not come find me and tell me about another guy she was dating. I hated small talk, and with her, I dreaded it even more because it was the same three topics that she always ranted on about. My mindset was to just get through the year, my last year. I gave up on developing any sort of ongoing meaningful friendships. I was not trying because, in all honesty, I did not care. All I wanted to focus on was showing up and doing whatever I had to do and leaving not a second after ten till three.

Throughout the years, I had other resource students in the majority of my classes. I had the paraprofessionals as well. It wasn't, however, helping me with attempting to avoid mind-numbing conversation topics and awkwardness. I was relatively okay with communicating with other resource students as long as the conversation was not mundane and pointless, which it was most of the time. What really bothered me was that, because of them being in there, paraprofessionals followed. I knew the paraprofessionals weren't exactly for me all the time, but I felt like everyone else associated me with needing the extra help. Like I was the dumb one. I knew I wasn't, but a paraprofessional hanging around felt like maybe I was. All of the other years prior, there were a couple of paraprofessionals that were more demanding than others, while a select few were more relaxed and made me feel good. I appreciated the good paraprofessionals.

My first-hour class was math; gotta love starting your day off with math, right? Along with the majority of students, it was not at all the best class of the day for the reason that math is complicated as hell. My teacher was known for running student council, and most of those kids, if not all of them were associated with the popular social circle. You might know where this is going; she seemed more comfortable with the students who were seemingly easier to initiate conversation with.

Around my junior/senior year of high school, I began to connect the dots and began to understand why it seems easier for teachers to communicate with other students. I became very aware of myself and the things that I did or did not do in school, and having so much awareness sometimes made it even more frustrating to not be able to connect the "how." Even now, as an adult, it is frustrating, and it is something that I have to continually examine and work through in order to be successful in everyday life.

My class did not consist of the most inclusive group of students, which made me dislike the class one hundred times more. It felt as if they were all in the popular group, all besides Heather and me, of course. We had a paraprofessional in the class for us, which I did not mind because math is an area that

I really struggled in, and I knew I needed the help. No matter how stubborn I wanted to be. The help I received was very much needed and is honestly the reason why I passed the class. Lesson: ask and accept help along the way.

The resource room, like any other year, was a safe place for me. I have my teacher to thank for that. She understood me in a way that was very comforting in an academic way, as well as understanding my emotional needs. She was aware of what I needed and provided advice and resources accordingly. Mrs. Robbins had more time to devote to her students because she had fewer students in one class period. The kids were not judgmental; we all needed a little help. There was a sense of safety that I did not feel in any other classroom. It was a nice change of environment for me. I thanked God for this safe landing each day.

My government class was also a class in which I felt as comfortable as I could be in a classroom. In a traditional classroom, anyway. Again, my teacher played a role in that, and I am grateful. He was the type of person who was nice to everybody regardless of their personality, which for me was a bonus. His understanding nature did not excuse the annoying jock students who loved the attention of being the class clowns. The teacher was not afraid to put them in their place, which was amusing. Something that stood out to me more than anything was his patience, and he seemed to genuinely want to build a relationship with me. These are great traits to have as a teacher, especially with someone like me in your classroom. I felt important and not INVISIBLE.

The teacher had this understanding of me without addressing the famous question of why. He allowed it to exist without making me feel different. This automatically made the environment so much more comfortable. I did not have to pretend to be anybody else because my teacher expected something different, a "normal" student. That did not seem to bother him, which meant more to me than he will ever know. I even felt comfortable enough to tell a story in front of the class. Later, at the parent-teacher conferences, he explained it as a "drop the mic" moment. I enjoyed his class for the most part, despite hard quizzes and tests. The real difference between this class and others was my teacher. Taking the time to understand your students is so important, and the patience that it takes, whether it is academic-related or not, is a trait all teachers need. He was one in a million.

My last class of the day was personal finance, which ended up being the most dreaded subject. The beginning started out like any other class, with the hatred of the subject matter. I did not know anything about money and did not have any interest in doing so. My teacher was intimidating, to say the least, both in her appearance as well as the way she spoke to her students. I was very wary of going into her class based on what I already knew, but my mom thought taking this class would benefit me.

My teacher was very direct and harsh in a way. Or it could just be the way in which she chose her words. Either way, my friends and I saw her as intimidating. I purposely kept my distance and only spoke when I absolutely had to, which was rare. Math did not come naturally to me, nor did the concept of money, besides spending it, of course. That class obviously had a lot of math involved, which made it difficult, and me being apprehensive about my teacher made it even more so.

You all know by now, I hate asking questions, and I hate it even more when I am uncomfortable in the environment.

For as far back as I can remember, I was really good at acting like I understood concepts when I really had no idea what the hell I was doing. I would act like I was actually doing my assignment by reading and rereading the directions and doodling and erasing. We had this assignment where we had to calculate earnings and deductions with no calculator. I had absolutely no idea what I was doing. I looked at the paper, read the directions, and that is about as far as I got until the last fifteen minutes of class. My teacher was walking by to see how all of us were doing. Like most of the rest of the class, I was struggling with it even though we had gone over the chapter contents in great detail.

The thing that is frustrating for most teachers is that it takes me a while to fully understand certain concepts. She was not the most patient teacher, which was another reason why I was hesitant in asking for help, and she was very direct in her choice of words. Something about the way in which she spoke or her subtle actions brought me back to Mr. King. Something about it reminded me of what had occurred while I was in that classroom, and that scared me. I cannot explain exactly how or why that worry and fear welled up inside me. I just know that it did, and it was a very real, intense feeling.

I believe it was a Wednesday, and ironically, that Thursday, we had parent-teacher conferences, and I did not go because it did not seem necessary. I told my mom my concerns, and she took them with her to discuss with the personal finance teacher. My teacher said she understood and that she would never want to make me feel like that. I was relieved when my mom came home afterwards and told me that. However, it showed me Mr. King's impact still haunted me five years later.

That weekend our family had a wedding to attend, my dad and I were driving to take my two dogs to the boarding kennel. Along our drive I recall a deep and heartfelt conversation I had with him. I explained the situation to him, and he looked over at me and said, "It is sad that he has affected you that much."

I paused, looking out the window, and said, "Yes, it is." I could feel the genuineness in his voice, and I believe for the first time, we both simultaneously recognized how real those wounds were.

Going back to school after spending a beautiful weekend in Colorado was something that I was dreading. Especially with the unknown of what would occur during my personal finance class or if anything would happen at all. When I got back, I felt extremely vulnerable, and it was an all-too-familiar feeling that I was not prepared for. I walked into class, somewhat afraid and not knowing what to expect. I remember trying my hardest to appear INVISIBLE, and I felt on edge.

Close to the end of class, something unexpected happened and I was quite surprised. The teacher came up to my desk and asked me, "Did your mom convince you that I don't hate you?"

I nervously chuckled and said, "Yes."

Then she leaned over and whispered, "You know, if a teacher really hates you, they will most likely ignore you instead of trying to help you." She then walked away and left me to ponder that statement.

The thing was, I knew she did not hate me. Despite her direct nature, I could see that she was not frustrated with me. She just did not understand me, or rather she just did not take the time to. It is so important to attempt the best you can to get to understand your students on an academic level as well as on an emotional level. The importance of this effort cannot be overestimated. That level of understanding will prevent you from running into clashes and misunderstandings with your students.

I was so done with school at that point, battling a major case of senioritis, which brought out the rebellion in me a little bit. There were specific classes which I knew I could easily get away with not being there or at least in certain circumstances anyway. I hit senioritis a little early. My whole senior year, I was just itching to get out, and I just got to the point where I did not care. Obviously, graduating high school was the big end goal that I could clearly see in sight, so I could not skip classes too often, but when I could, I took advantage.

Towards the end of the semester, I was getting excited because it would be my last semester in school, which made me incredibly happy to think about. Woven into the excitement was also anxiety and sadness because, within about a week of finals, I learned that my resource teacher was leaving. Not at the end of the year, but at that time.

I was in my weights class standing by the door, watching the clock tick as it got closer to 10:15, when class got out, and a girl who had her as an English teacher came to tell me she was leaving. I thought she was kidding at first. Not until she started crying did I realize she was serious. "She was going to tell you next hour, but I needed to tell somebody first," she said with a sad tone of voice.

I had resource room as a class next hour, and I was not prepared to hear this news. Even though the resource teacher was going to say what I already knew, hearing those words come out of her own mouth left me feeling sick to my stomach.

When the bell rang, instant anxiety and dread surged throughout my entire body and I did not want to go into class. I just wanted to run and hide. Mrs. Robbins told all of us as soon as the bell rang for class to begin, and hearing her say the reality out loud made my heart feel like it dropped all the way down to my feet. After she told us, the atmosphere almost immediately changed within the classroom. Deep down, I was filled with sadness and anger.

For the rest of the class period, I was quiet, which was unusual for that class, and attempted to not let my true emotions show. I was angry because I did not understand why she could not just power through and get through the remaining semester. Mainly for selfish reasons, because I only had one semester. If I could get through one more semester, she easily could too. I felt betrayed that she could just leave that easily and leave me to figure out my last semester by myself. It was as if she was abandoning me. In reality, I knew she was not leaving me personally, but it sure as hell felt that way.

You have to understand something: when you are as vulnerable as I was in school, you rarely find teachers who understand you. To me, Mrs. Robbins was more than a teacher; she was someone who understood me and did not judge me, and that meant a lot. Since finding teachers who I connected with was so rare, the news hit harder than some. Even though I had only one semester left, that fear of lack of connection with a teacher scared me because it was really important to me to have that.

I am forever grateful that my parents never really got onto me about grades. Once in awhile, it was warranted, but they both had the attitude of "as long as you are doing what you are supposed to and trying your best, that is all you can do." I believe they saw the effort I put in, which eased the somewhat shocked looks on their faces when they received my report card. My grades were not awful, but for the work I put in on finals, I believe I should have gotten better grades, which seems to be the story of my life.

The last day before Christmas break, before the bell rang to signal freedom, Mrs. Robbins gave all of us an individualized handwritten letter, which I appreciated a lot. It was hard for me to realize she would not be back for the second semester, but I was busy convincing myself it would not be that bad and everything would be okay.

The resource room shifted a little bit with receiving a new teacher, which was an interesting change. He was totally different from Mrs. Robbins; it was just a different feeling that I got from him. I feel like he was just there to be there, to just fill in if you will. His personality was very laid-back, almost to the point of actually not caring. It would have been worse if it was more than one semester, but since it was my last, it did not really matter as much as I thought it would. I was just focused on getting out of there. Each day of school was another closer to graduation.

I got out of school at eleven every day, which was great for about the first month. I had the opportunity to just do whatever I wanted for about ten days or so, and then the boredom set in. I did not have many real friends, so hanging out with friends after the school day or school morning was not really an option. I was so bored that I forced myself to get a job, which was probably a good thing looking back. It forced me to be around other people. Having people to occupy my time after the school day was a good thing for me. And I was making money, always a plus.

Pretty quickly, my routine became going to work after school, which I felt gave me a purpose. The rest of my life was relatively the same at that point.

There was a point as it got closer to the end of the year where we had a lot of "meetings" regarding the logistics of graduation. Those meetings were usually held at the end of the day, so this particular day all of the senior class got called to the cafeteria. I usually skipped these kinds of things, but I refrained from the temptation. Knowing what I was doing on that day was important. I sat at the table farthest from the big crowd with one earbud in my ear, waiting for what was going to be said. As best I could, I was trying to block out all the extra background noise so I could get out of there as fast as possible. Being in a room with all of these students who immediately ran to their friend groups made it super awkward and uncomfortable for me. I simply didn't have one.

The principal was talking about how graduation would go regarding seating and walking. I expected to hear what I already was dreading to hear, which would include us walking in partners. Turned out I was pleasantly surprised with what came out her mouth. "We are not going to have partners this year; it will all be in alphabetical order." If I could have screamed in that moment, I would have; instead, I smiled and felt this sense of peace wash through my whole body.

Dr. Kuhlman, the principal, continued, "The reasoning for this is so we can avoid feelings getting hurt." She understood that kids like me would not have anyone to walk with during graduation. I didn't even have anyone to ask. There was nothing that made me happier than hearing that. I personally believed it would cause unnecessary work and stress for everybody involved. It brought me the biggest sigh of relief.

To my principal, thank you. You recognized me and other students in that school that others may not even have thought twice about. Thank you for taking our vulnerabilities into consideration. It made me feel like I was recognized and heard without saying a single word. A couple of months later I would be graduating, which I could not believe. High school really does go by fast, faster than you think.

On May 22, 2017, I graduated from high school. Graduation symbolized so much more than receiving a diploma. Of course, it was a celebratory moment for all of us, but it was really an amazing moment for me. It was a celebration of my own strength, courage, and perseverance, which meant more to me than any piece of paper. I was and still am proud of all I have accomplished. All that hardship was so worth it, and seeing my parents so proud made me realize that none of it mattered anymore. It was time to feel pride. A building with four walls and rooms full of teachers and students would not define me.

Nothing was more satisfying than hearing my name called as I crossed the stage. Hearing my dad scream, in dead silence, "I love you, Murphy," as I crossed the stage, gave me an instant smile on my face, and my heart was filled with so much joy. It was also a kind of moment where we all looked at each other and had an "oh my God, she did it" realization. I could see it in my parents' faces, and that is a moment I will never forget.

When I say that whatever you were in school does not matter anymore, I say it with all honesty. You can change your story into a positive one. You have the ability to shift your perspective and start over. I promise.

It is time to define yourself, and not let others do it for you. It won't be easy, but it never is.

CHAPTER 13

Graduation and Beyond

The moment I stepped off that stage, I quickly realized that I was no longer trapped. I was free! The freedom that swept through me felt euphoric and amazing. There was this initial excitement that lasted a couple of days. Quickly after that, it hit me. I realized it was now my responsibility to create my own life for myself and that scared me a little bit. Being in school, through the thirteen years that you attend, seems to last forever. Which is why it is so difficult for students to imagine themselves anywhere outside of the world surrounding textbooks and classrooms.

It might be shocking, but there is more to life than the exciting countdown to summer and moving on to the next grade level. There are many emotions relating to that fact, at least there was for me. Don't get me wrong; school was awful, but there is also this odd sense of comfort that surrounds it. To have that routine and sense of simplicity stripped away takes a while for anybody to get used to. The one part that I loved was the inherent structure.

After many students graduate high school, they reflect. Even if you say you couldn't care less, you still do even if you really don't want to. Even if it hurts more than anything else.

I could not help but reflect on my school experience, and throughout that bout of reflection, I learned a lot.

What I found interesting and which is often quite true for introverts is that we enjoy other people's presence just to listen. I was entertained by the conversations had by other students, just listening, never chiming in. The ultimate observer.

For a while, I thought the smart thing to do was to attend college because that was what you do after high school. That is seemingly what you are supposed to do, right? After the hounding from my school counselor, I got that belief drilled into my head that this was what I *HAD* to do. As I am years out of school now, I am realizing how unjust that belief really is. It turns out your whole world will not fall apart if you don't receive a tearful goodbye from your parents in your perfectly decorated dorm room.

It took me two years to be ready to face a classroom again, without wanting to die at the thought of it. I was still working, which kept me busy, and that was nice as it allowed me to socialize somewhat. After about six months working at a grocery store, I actually met somebody who I can confidently categorize as a friend. It made work a little bit more fun, as fun as bagging groceries could get at least.

Along with trying to expand my social circle, I pretty quickly had to figure out what I wanted to do when it came to school. Many people told me that none of the things that happen in high school really matter after high school. I never believed that until it happened to me. They were all right. None of it matters. Once you receive your diploma and walk out those doors, everything from there on out is fresh. A new level of independence is enticing yet unnerving. None of those people matter anymore; your friends, you can keep, if you feel so inclined. I never had true friends in high school, just acquaintances that I tended to cross paths with. It was time to start over.

Not being around a lot of kids your own age takes a toll on you after a while. Not having the best social skills in the world makes it even harder. Introverts like me struggle with properly communicating to others, sometimes even with good friends. As well as my lack of social skills, a perfect storm for loneliness began to manifest.

After two years of working different jobs and figuring out what my place was in this world, I made a big decision. I was going to move to a small town twenty minutes away from my home and attend a community college. The night before I left, I posted this message on social media:

> I never ever thought I would go to college. Ever. Not because of the lack of effort gaining an education entails; rather, it was the all-consuming trauma that fled through my veins every time I mentioned the word 'school.' I am ready now. I am ready and willing to get uncomfortable. I am willing to feel for the first time in a long time. I feel like a whole new person. To that person who wants to give up or who is afraid to go against societal norms of going to college straight out of high school—it is so worth the wait. Your mental health matters. Your physical health matters. Let me tell you ... It is okay. It is more than okay. You are not broken. You are doing what is best for you and that in itself is a win much greater than anything in this world.

Life is full of ups and downs for everyone. Our experiences shape us without us even realizing it. My life continues to have highs and lows, and I will handle them with the lessons of my experiences. It will be okay.

CHAPTER **14**

Ten Things I Wish Teachers Knew About Me

1. Don't look away! Don't ignore those kids that are harder to connect with. While some kids may not want to be in the spotlight. No one, and I mean *no one*, truly wants to be invisible. A smile can take some kids through an entire day.

   It is easy—simply look them in the eye. Don't get distracted by the easy-to-talk-to kids. Look at those who won't look back. Say hello and smile. Mean it, and do it over and over and over again. Eventually, even the tough ones will start to smile back. If they don't, know they feel it on the inside. Let that be enough. Know you are making a difference, even if you can't see it.

2. A teacher can change a child's story. This starts with *intentional* conversations. Have them frequently, with eye contact and a genuine tone. Keep up with this consistent effort. It is worth it, even if as a teacher you are uncomfortable at first because a child may not respond in the typical way.

   You truly seeing a child makes it more possible for other kids to accept. Intention is the difference here. Make an effort to seek information and share information. Teachers are in schools to teach us more than what the day's lessons are. You can change a child's life in whichever way you choose. Make it count, make it good. Don't let your name be the negative teacher a child thinks of at graduation. It is completely in your control.

3. **Don't underestimate the power of a "Hello"! There were teachers who would look at me and say hello. It was enough for me to feel safe and to feel like they might actually like me. You would be surprised how many teachers do not make an effort with kids who are uncomfortable making eye contact, therefore making it easy to be INVISIBLE.**

    Acknowledgment is something I always looked for in teachers. I did not have very many friends (acquaintances), so to have teachers give me the time of day was often welcome. Some students have absolutely no one to turn to, and nice gestures, like a hello, can mean the world. That smile, combined with extra patience and understanding, provides us a little breathing room and safety. Nice gestures teachers made, whether verbal or nonverbal, made me feel as though I could break down my walls a little bit. It is important to provide safety for your students. Whether you know it or not, you provide more than you even realize.

4. **Beware of the bullies, and be careful *not* to become one of them!**

    Most teachers seem to forget this very true statement. I do not blame you. There is no possible way to know everything that is going on daily in the classroom, but it is possible to become more aware of the effects of bullying, emotional and physical. How do students act in the classroom? Does it seem as if they are afraid of their peers? Awareness creates change. I had some instances where I overhead the talkative student—I, the person who just took what was dished out. This one kid who I had always had issues with ended up traveling with me to high school. In middle school, in one of my classes, he called me retarded. Not a good choice of words.

I, deciding for once to stand up for myself, told him to fuck off while the teacher was walking towards me. Not wise either. She looked shocked and said, "Murphy, that's not very nice."

Nobody expects the quiet girl to stand up for herself. I do understand that endorsing such behavior is not necessarily acceptable, but between the two students it would be quite apparent who started it. Pay attention to the possible initiators, as well as possible victims. There need to be consequences for such behavior, and you have the power to do so.

5. **Spend the first few minutes of class at the door or inside, making connections. This is a challenging few minutes for kids like me, and it is a guaranteed anxiety-ridden start if the teacher is outside chatting with other teachers. We need you. Don't let the opportunity pass.**

Teachers often have a hard time differentiating general shyness from disengagement and anxiety. There is a lot that happens in middle school and high school classrooms when the teacher is not there. Please be there for these kids. This isn't a time for freedom. It is actually a time for modeling, connection, and kindness. These interactions impact how much a child will be able to listen, how much effort they put in, and how they see each other. The impact is far-reaching.

6. **The impact of a teacher can be felt for years and may make you believe things about yourself that just aren't true! Never let someone else's negative opinion, even a teacher's, determine who you are or who you will be!**

    You are more than just a teacher! Your verbal and nonverbal actions speak loudly. Know that the impact is sometimes permanent. There are teachers we remember for the love, kindness, and teaching they displayed each day. There are teachers we don't remember at all. Then there is the teacher whose negative actions are so impactful, they are permanently felt. Which teacher will you be today?

7. **Nothing is more important than having a safe space at school. The hope is that all classrooms are safe places. Teachers' reactions, verbal and nonverbal, make the difference.**

    We are all watching you, even if it appears we are not. I may remember your laid- back personality, your humor, your respectful nature. I also will remember the way you taught, but what I'll remember the most is the way you interacted with all of us. I will remember the ways you attempted to make genuine conversation. The times you gave me positive reinforcement. I will also remember the times when you were cold and just focused on the students that gave *you* the most attention.

8. **A teacher showing students respect is a sign of strength, not weakness!**

I am not a particularly sensitive person; I obviously have my moments. I am only human. I can easily tell the difference between frustration, flat-out anger, and tough love. I understand why others are reacting the way they are and can put emotions into the right context. Some people on the spectrum have trouble identifying emotions and facial expressions in connection to said feelings. I have never really had that trait. It probably helped with continuous critiques by my coaches as well as some teachers. Despite that, understanding strong emotions from my teachers and coaches was hard for me to swallow.

I care a lot about what people think of me, and I wanted to be seen as independent and strong, not weak. Being in the school environment was always a vulnerable place that made communication with teachers a task. I have a hyperawareness that is important for staff members to recognize. They should speak to their students accordingly, making conversations seem less daunting. In the classroom, it made a world of difference to have even just a few select teachers who recognized that; it brought needed comfort. It made a difference in the way I communicated with them as well as enhancing the possibility of sharing a part of myself. Opening up was an added bonus. Be careful in the way in which you speak with those students who may need more attention and patience. Comfort is what we are searching for.

9. **While you may not be the cause of a student's anxiety, it is in your power to reduce it. Reach out, build the relationships, talk to students about normal topics. If you can't do it naturally, this is the time to fake it. Building relationships breaks down anxiety for everyone.**

    You have the power to lift up, bend, or break. Anxiety is a real thing for students. If a student is struggling with depression or anxiety, it is not your fault. Don't take it personally. It is a teacher's responsibility to not ignore these signs, which inevitably makes it worse. Be there, reach out. Know students are bending and possibly breaking. Help support them and lift them up!

10. **Be generous with compliments, even if you don't mean them at first! This draws students out and is the beginning of a relationship. When you get to know a student (especially the hard-to-get-to-know ones), you can then give actual genuine compliments. Don't be shy in letting them and their parents know. The return you will get in a student's effort and attention just might surprise you.**

    Truly believe that all kids are worthy of compliments. All kids deserve it for something. Not just the kid who made the touchdown, who sang the lead in the play, or who won the debate. When you truly believe all kids are good enough, be prepared to show it relentlessly, every day. The difference is between giving help and doing harm.

These are the main things I wish teachers knew. I wish I had had someone to explain this to all my teachers because it would have made a hell of a difference. Teachers are human. All I am asking is for you to at least try. It may seem easy. Actually, common sense is not as easy as it might seem. It is easier to just ignore matters and have someone else deal with the kids who are not your cookie-cutter straight-A students. When a student gets in trouble for speaking too loudly or being defiant, you can send them to the principal's office. The students who seem to be speaking too softly, if at all, and you're feeling like you are talking to a wall when you try to explain a concept, don't have that simple of an answer. All kids are looking for someone who believes in them. Someone who sees more potential than what can be seen on the surface. Take these main points. Absorb the ones you do not resonate with. Keep the ones you do in the back of your mind to refresh on when you need them.

To the students who are reading this and are in awe that your words seemed to magically appear on this page, I see you. I hear you, and I can only hope that my words can enforce change and not just be read and never looked at again until you decide to deep-clean your bookshelf. This book is for you as well. When I was younger, I wished something like this had been put out there, so I could be understood. Now I am writing this for you. No explanation; just words on a page with real experiences attached to them. Nothing dramatic, but real life. My hope is that it can help you feel less alone in your journey.

CHAPTER **15**

Advice for Students Like Me!

For other students:

1. I am stronger than I thought! So are you!!
2. I can do a lot more than others thought I could!
3. I should not have cared as much about what people thought of me. Others' assumptions DO NOT MATTER.
4. Quality over quantity is what matters in friendship, regardless of whether high school makes you feel differently.
5. Standing up for yourself is not a crime. Just do it in a way that keeps you from having regrets.
6. Self-acceptance is a huge part of your own healing. You are good enough just the way you are. Your younger self made mistakes, and that is okay. There is a place for you in this world.
7. Follow your gut on everything that you know in your heart. Pursue it!
8. You don't have to follow the crowd; do what's best for you!

It is no secret that school has had a huge influence on my life, unfortunately not because of my positive experiences. My negative experiences were a combination of my own personal struggles with PDD-NOS, anxiety, depression, eating disorders, and teachers and other students along the way who just did not have the tools and understanding to help me break free from the challenges. There were good ones along the way, thank goodness, but not enough.

I think of a school where there are all Mrs. Endicotts, Mrs. Gawiths, Mrs. Fergusons, Mr. Fosters, Mrs. Jennings, Mrs. Jenkins, Mrs. Huschers, Mrs. Lichtis, Mrs. Ryans, Mr. Cornelsens, Mr. Hagers, and Mr. Dusenberys who take the time with the kids like me. How lucky we all would be. A school where there are kids who look all kids in the eye and genuinely say hello, simply make eye contact, scoot over and invite another to sit down or go to lunch, make conversation, and include with acceptance. What a world it would be. I am not saying everyone needs to be best friends or everyone is perfect, but wow, what a world it would be if we tried.

CPSIA information can be obtained
at www.ICGtesting.com
Printed in the USA
LVHW100641141222
735195LV00002B/323